FILE

MW01178765

MICROSOFT
WORKS
FOR WINDOWS 95

PUBLISHED BY

Microsoft Press
A Division of Microsoft Corporation
One Microsoft Way
Redmond, Washington 98052-6399

Library of Congress Cataloging-in-Publication Data
Field guide to Microsoft Works for Windows 95.
      p.   cm.
   Includes index.
   ISBN 1-55615-895-5

   1. Integrated software. 2. Microsoft Works for Windows.
I. Siechert & Wood, Inc.
QA76.76.I57F55   1995
005.369--dc20   95-35901
                                                      CIP

Printed and bound in the United States of America.

1 2 3 4 5 6 7 8 9 QBP 9 8 7 6 5 4

Distributed to the book trade in Canada by Macmillan of
Canada, a division of Canada Publishing Corporation.

A CIP catalogue record for this book is available from the
British Library.

Microsoft Press books are available through
booksellers and distributors worldwide. For further
information about international editions, contact your local
Microsoft Corporation office. Or contact Microsoft Press
International directly at fax (206) 936-7329.

Acquisitions Editor: Lucinda Rowley

Project Editor: John Pierce

Writer: Carl Siechert

FIELD GUIDE TO

MICROSOFT
WORKS
FOR WINDOWS 95

Siechert & Wood, Inc.

The Field Guide to Microsoft Works version 4 for Windows 95 is divided into four sections. These sections are designed to help you find the information you need quickly.

1 ENVIRONMENT

Terms and ideas you'll want to know to get the most out of Works. All the basic parts of Works are shown and explained. The emphasis here is on quick answers, but most topics are cross-referenced so you can find out more if you want to.

Diagrams of key window components, with quick definitions, cross referenced to more complete information.

Tipmeister

Watch for me as you use this Field Guide. I'll point out helpful hints and let you know what to watch for.

15 WORKS A TO Z

An alphabetic list of commands, tasks, terms, and procedures.

Cross references to related topics.

Definitions of key concepts and terms, and examples showing you why you should know them.

Quick identification of icons and Works modules.

Step-by-step guides to performing most Works tasks.

165 TROUBLESHOOTING

A guide to common problems—how to avoid them, and what to do when they occur.

175 QUICK REFERENCE

A full list of tools that you can use to customize your toolbar for fast access to features in Works.

187 INDEX

Complete reference to all elements of the Field Guide.

INTRODUCTION

··

*In the field and on expedition, you need practical
solutions. Fast. This field guide provides just these
sorts of lightning quick answers. But take two
minutes now and read the introduction. It explains
how this unusual little book works.*

WHAT IS A FIELD GUIDE?

A Field Guide—to North American Forests, to Equatorial Africa, or to Microsoft Works—is a pocket-sized handbook that provides quick, short, and easy-to-use answers for those pesky questions that come up when you're trying to get about your work.

This Field Guide to Microsoft Works is different from all the other computer books on the shelf. Its illustrations work like road maps that point you exactly to the information you need. If you're a new user, the Field Guide gives you step-by-step instructions that will have you using Works like a pro in no time. If you're an experienced user, the Field Guide provides you with a concise quick reference to all the Works terms, tasks, and techniques.

WHEN YOU HAVE A QUESTION

When you have a question about how to do something with Works, turn to the Field Guide's Environment section. The Environment works like an illustrated index. For example, if you want to know how to work with a database, flip to pages 10 and 11, and you'll see an illustration of a Works database. The captions for the different parts of the picture describe all the things you can do with databases and point you to the exact entries in the Works A to Z section that describe each task in detail.

WHEN YOU WANT TO KNOW MORE

The second part of the Field Guide, Works A to Z, is like an illustrated dictionary to Microsoft Works. It contains more than 200 entries in alphabetical order that describe terms and give you the steps to perform tasks. (Often, you'll be able to turn directly to Works A to Z to find the information you need.) For example, to learn how to have Works dial the phone for you, read the **Dialing Phone Numbers** entry.

WHEN YOU HAVE A PROBLEM

The third section of the Field Guide, Troubleshooting, is where to turn when something doesn't work the way it seems like it should. This section of the Field Guide describes the most common problems that new or casual Works users come across, and gives you one or more solutions to fix each problem.

HINTS FOR USING THIS FIELD GUIDE

This Field Guide uses several conventions to help you find your way around:

- When you see a task or term in **boldface**, it means you can find information about that task or term in the Works A to Z section.

- When you see the ⁘ symbol followed by a term or task, it means that term or task in the Works A to Z section contains some additional information related to the topic at hand.

- Throughout this Field Guide, you'll see these four icons: 🖋️🖥️🗄️💬. They are the same icons you see on the Works Tools tab of the **Works Task Launcher**. They tell you which of Works' four modules and document types—Word Processor, Spreadsheet, Database, or Communications—a term or task applies to.

- In some places in this Field Guide, you'll see tools like this: 🖨️. The tool illustrations show you a shortcut way to perform a task: click its button on the toolbar. (To change the tool buttons that appear on your toolbar, check out **Customizing Toolbars** in the Works A to Z section of this Field Guide.)

ENVIRONMENT

Need to get the lay of the land quickly? Then the Environment is the place to start. It defines the key terms you'll need to know and the core ideas you should understand as you begin exploring Microsoft Works.

THE WORKS TASK LAUNCHER

The Works Task Launcher first appears when you start Microsoft Works. You'll summon it often because it provides a signpost that points the way to many features in Works and to the documents you create with Works.

Click the TaskWizards tab when you want to use a **TaskWizard**. TaskWizards guide you through the process of creating a specialized document, such as a letterhead, or performing a task, such as a **mail merge**.

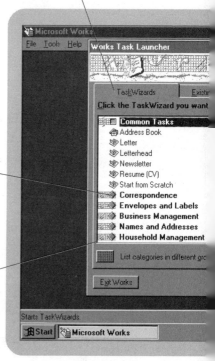

Click a category to open it, and then click a TaskWizard name to see its description. If it's the one you want, click OK to proceed.

Select User Defined Templates from the list when you want to create a new document based on a stored **template**, a "skeleton" document that can save you time and promote consistency among your documents.

Letterheads

Actually, the very first time you start Works, you'll see a welcome screen that gives you an opportunity to take a guided tour of Works. Click OK to take the tour if you like. But if you're adventuresome—and you wouldn't have bought this book if you weren't, right? —click Cancel to skip the tour; you can see it later by choosing the

Help Introduction To Works command.

Your Works session then begins with the **Works Task Launcher.** The **dialog box** goes away after you use it, but you can bring it back by clicking the Task Launcher tool on the **toolbar.**

Starting Works

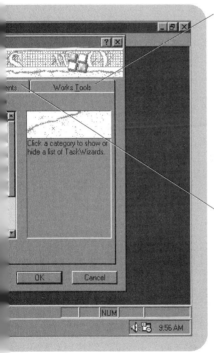

Click the Works Tools tab when you want to create a new document. Then click the button for the document type you want to create—Word Processor, Spreadsheet, Database, or Communications.

Works maintains a list of the last eight documents you've used. To reuse one of them, click the Existing Documents tab, and then double-click the document's name in the list. You can also quickly access existing files that are not in the recently-used list; click Open A Document Not Listed Here.

Finding Files

THE WORKS APPLICATION WINDOW

The documents you use in Works appear in the Works application window. Within the application window, you can open up to eight documents at one time.

The menu bar lists the commands you can choose. To choose a command, click the menu name and then, when the menu drops down, click the command name.

:•: **Exiting Works; Opening Documents; Printing; Saving Documents**

Each window—whether it's an application window or a document window—has a Control menu that lets you move the window, change its size, or close it. Click the Control-menu icon to open the Control menu.

:•: **Closing Documents; Control-Menu Commands; Resizing Windows**

The **insertion point** shows where the next character you type will appear.

The **workspace** defines your Works application window, including its size and screen position, and the names and window sizes of all open documents. If you save the workspace settings, Works restores the settings the next time you start the program.

:•: **Options; Saving the Workspace**

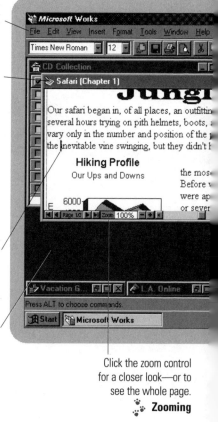

Click the zoom control for a closer look—or to see the whole page.

:•: **Zooming**

If you've used other Windows-based applications, you'll find your way around the Works **application window** in no time.

Within its confines, you can open up to eight **document windows.** Each

document window contains a single Works **document**, which can be from any Works module: word processor, spreadsheet (and charting), database, or communications.

One way to move or copy information—within a document, between documents, or even between applications—is via the **Clipboard**. The toolbar includes tools for common Clipboard operations: **Cutting, Copying,** and **Pasting**.

Drag and Drop; Sharing Works Data

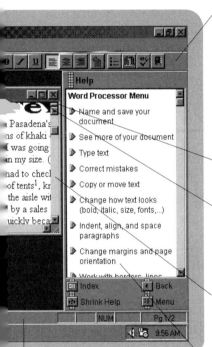

The tools on the **toolbar** provide shortcuts for frequently used commands. Instead of choosing a command from a menu, you simply click the tool. Works uses a different toolbar for each module; each toolbar includes only tools that are appropriate to use with the active document window.

Customizing Toolbars

Drag the split bar to divide a document window into **window panes.**

Click a document window's minimize button to reduce the window to an icon at the bottom of the workspace—getting it out of your way without closing the document.

Scroll bars appear when a document won't fit in its window; click them to view other parts of the document.

Scrolling

Works offers **help** about the module you're currently using. Click the buttons in the help window for more information—or to hide the help when you know it all.

The **status bar** provides helpful information about using commands and about the active document.

WORD PROCESSOR DOCUMENTS

The Works word processor module not only lets you process words, but you can add charts, tables, pictures, and other elements to embellish those words.

The **ruler** lets you see and modify the indent and tab-stop settings for the current paragraph.
⋰ **Indents and Alignment; Margins; Page Setup; Tabs**

Your pages can include **headers and footers**, which you can use to print **page numbers**. You might also want to include the date and **time**.

Probably the most important thing in a word processor document is the words.
⋰ **Copying Text; Deleting Text; Drag and Drop; Editing Text; Entering Text; Moving Text; Replacing Text; Selecting Text; Undo**

You can insert **charts** or other objects anywhere in your document.
⋰ **Adding Pictures; Embedding and Linking Existing Objects; Embedding New Objects; OLE Linking and Embedding**

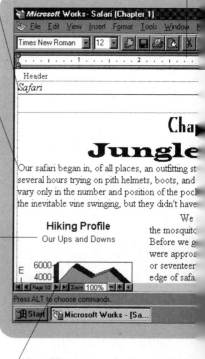

View different parts of a document by clicking the page buttons or the scroll bars.
⋰ **Bookmarks; Finding Text; Go To; Scrolling**

At its core, the word processor module is a very capable processor of words and text. It offers extensive text **formatting** options, a built-in **spelling checker**, automatic **bulleted lists**, multiple **text columns**, and powerful search-and-replace capabilities. But the word processor module is also the best place to see how Works integrates information from different modules: You can embed a chart or table from the spreadsheet module, a picture from the **ClipArt Gallery** or Microsoft **Draw**, or even a pop-up reminder from **Note-It**.

You can use a variety of **fonts** in your Works documents.
　✿ **Changing Fonts; Points; WordArt**

Paragraph-formatting options let you control the appearance of **paragraphs** and ensure that certain paragraphs stay on the same page.
　✿ **Paragraph Breaks**

Whether you write for a professional journal or just letters home to Mom, you can use features such as **footnotes** and **endnotes**.

Works can smooth out ragged edges by hyphenating words.
　✿ **Ending Lines; Hyphenation; Nonbreaking Spaces; Word Wrap**

Your friends and colleagues don't have Works? Not to worry. You can import and export documents for **Microsoft Word**, **WordPerfect**, **WordPad**, and **Write**.
　✿ **Exporting Documents**

What about business documents?

Works has you covered, whether you want to print **letterheads**, **envelopes**, or **mailing labels**. And you can use **mail merge** to incorporate information from a Works database.

SPREADSHEET DOCUMENTS

The spreadsheet module simulates an accountant's ruled ledger sheets, but you don't need a green eyeshade to quickly and easily perform complex calculations on numbers.

The **entry bar** shows the **formula** or **value** in the active cell.
∴ **Calculating Formulas**

A cell is identified by its **column** letter and **row** number.
∴ **Cell Address; Names; Range**

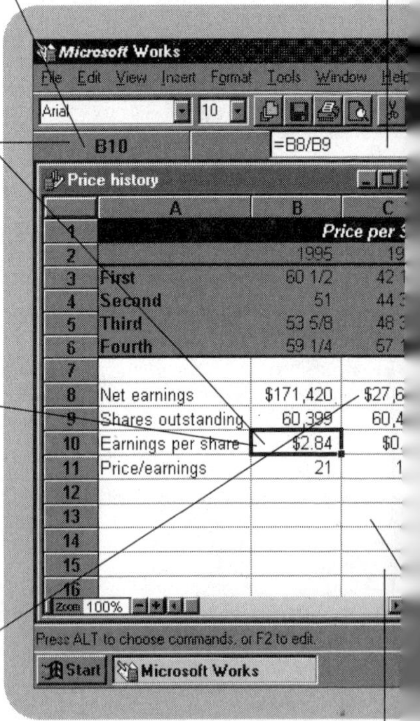

The **active cell** has a heavy border (the **cell selector**), and its address appears to the left of the entry bar.
∴ **Selecting Cells; Selecting Columns and Rows**

Numbers or formulas you enter always go in the active cell.
∴ **Editing Cells; Entering Numbers; Filling Cells; Fill Series**

Formatting numbers lets you display numeric information in a convenient and familiar form, including **fractions**, **percentages**, and **scientific notation**.
∴ **Alignment; Currency Symbols; Date Formats; Time Formats**

You can change the overall appearance of a spreadsheet in many ways. You can adjust the **column width**, **row height**, and **margins**. Or add **headers and footers**, including **page numbers**.
∴ **AutoFormatting; Gridlines**

8

The spreadsheet module is a whiz at performing mathematical calculations. And it can present the numbers in the form of colorful **charts**, which can enhance understanding of the numbers even among right-brained people.

The spreadsheet is a grid of rectangles called **cells**. The cells are where you put numeric **values** or **formulas** that perform calculations.

Formulas can also include **functions**, which let you perform complex calculations.
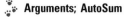 **Arguments; AutoSum**

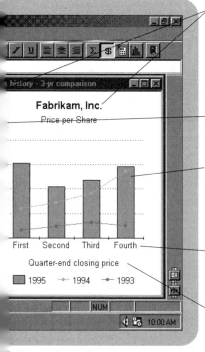

You can change the appearance of information in spreadsheets and charts by **changing fonts**.
Bold Characters; Italic Characters; Points; Underline Characters

You can highlight cells by adding **borders** and **shading**.

Works can create **charts** based on spreadsheet information.
Chart Formatting; Chart Types; Editing Charts

Chart text that accompanies a chart can include titles, axis labels, and legends.

You can embed Works spreadsheets and charts in word processor documents and database **forms**.
Exporting Documents; Lotus 1-2-3; Microsoft Excel; Sharing Works Data

You can change the arrangement of a spreadsheet's rows and columns.
Deleting Columns and Rows; Inserting Columns and Rows; Sorting Rows

DATABASE DOCUMENTS

The Works database can keep track of information—lists of customers or friends, store inventory, baseball card collections, and so on.

The information about each item in your database constitutes a **record**. In **list view**, each record occupies one row; in **form view**, only a single record is visible.

❖ **Adding Records; Deleting Records; Editing Records; Go To**

Each record is divided into **fields**, each holding a single piece of information.

❖ **Adding Fields; Deleting Fields; Hiding Fields**

In form view, the active field is indicated by reversing its colors; in list view, the active field is highlighted with a heavy border.

❖ **Selecting Cells; Selecting Columns and Rows**

Dress up your **forms** by **adding pictures**, **charts**, or objects from **WordArt**, **ClipArt Gallery**, **Draw**, or **Note-It**.

❖ **Embedding and Linking Existing Objects; Embedding New Objects; OLE Linking and Embedding**

You can add **borders** and **shading** to the background of fields, labels, or the entire form.

To the right of each **field name**, a **field line** shows you where to enter data.

❖ **Entering Data; Filling Cells; Fill Series**

You view and modify the information in the database module, but you can also merge database information into a word processor document—handy for **envelopes**, **mailing labels**, and other **mail merge** projects. The database module offers two basic views of your data: **form view**, which emulates a paper input form, and **list view**, which displays data in a spreadsheet-like tabular format. It has two other views: **form design view** lets you create forms, and **report view** allows you to sort and select records based on criteria you specify.

The **entry bar** shows the **value** or **formula** in the active field. Formulas can also include **functions**, which let you perform complex calculations.

To add a text element to a **form**, switch to **form design view**, move the **insertion point**, and then type.

∴ **Positioning Fields;**
   Resizing Fields

You can change the appearance of information in a database by **changing fonts**. You can apply different formatting in each **view**.

Formatting numbers lets you display numeric information in a convenient and familiar form.

∴ **Alignment**

You can protect certain fields from inadvertant changes.

∴ **Protecting Fields**

A **report** produces printed output that includes only the fields you want, sorts and groups records, and can include calculations such as the number of records in each group, the total value of a certain field, and so on.

∴ **Report View; Sorting Records**

A filter lets you find certain records and hides records that don't match your criteria. Hidden records are not included in database views, reports, or mail merge operations.

∴ **Filtering Records; Finding**
   Records; Hiding Records

COMMUNICATIONS DOCUMENTS

The Works communications module lets you use a modem and a telephone line to connect to online services, electronic bulletin boards, and other computers running a similar communications program.

Before you begin a communications session, you must establish various settings that match your modem's capabilities and the settings used by the computer you want to connect to.

Communication Settings; Phone Settings; Protocol; Terminal Settings

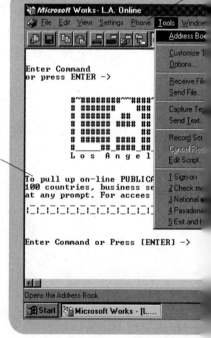

The document window shows text that you send and receive during a communications session.

Capturing Text; Sending and Receiving Text

You can also send any file that you have saved on disk to the other computer, or receive a file from the other computer. When you do so, a message box appears that monitors the progress of the file transfer; the actual file contents never appear on your screen.

Sending and Receiving Files

A communications document isn't made up of information that you type in a document window. Instead, a communications "document" stores all the information necessary to make a connection to a particular online service, along with any **scripts** you create. (The information that you send or receive during a communications session is discarded at the end of the session unless you save it to a file.) The commands to enter the connection information are all on the Settings menu.

To connect to another computer, choose the Phone Easy Connect command, click the **Easy Connect** toolbar button, or choose the Tools Sign-on command.

✥ Dialing Phone Numbers

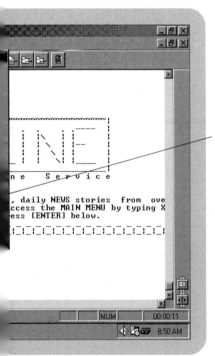

You can automate repetitive communications tasks by recording your actions as a **script**. After you record (and edit, if necessary) a script, you play it back by choosing its name from the Tools menu.

WORKS A TO Z

Maybe it's not a jungle out there. But you'll still want to keep a survival kit close at hand. Works A to Z, which starts on the next page, is just such a survival kit. It lists in alphabetic order the tools, terms, and techniques you'll need to know.

Absolute Cell References

An absolute cell reference describes a specific location in a spreadsheet. An absolute reference always refers to the same **cell** regardless of where in the spreadsheet you move or copy the cell that contains the reference. To create an absolute reference, use a dollar sign before the column letter and row number, like this: A1.

Press F4 to switch

When you enter a **formula**, you can insert a reference to a **cell** or a **range** by pointing. While the referenced cells are still highlighted, you can press F4 to switch among **relative cell references, mixed cell references**, and **absolute cell references.**

Active Cell

The active cell is the spreadsheet **cell** or database **field** that you are currently working with. It is the cell in which the text, numbers, or **formulas** you type are entered. The active cell has a highlighted border around it, and its address appears in the left portion of the **entry bar.**

Adding Fields

You can add a **field** to a database in either **form design view** or **list view**.

Adding a Field in Form Design View

To add a field in form design view, follow these steps:

1 **Right-click** where you want the new field.
2 Choose Insert Field from the **shortcut menu.**

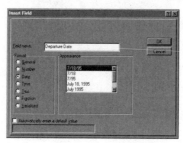

3 Type a name for the new field, select a format, and select appearance options. Then click OK.

The Insert Field dialog box closes, and your form reappears with the new field highlighted. You can now use the usual techniques for **positioning fields** and **resizing fields.**

Adding a Field in List View

To add a field in list view, follow these steps:

1 Right-click in the field next to where you want the new field.

2 From the shortcut menu, choose Insert Field and then choose Before (to insert the new field to the left of the field you clicked) or After (to insert the new field to the right).

3 Type a name for the new field, select a format, and select appearance options. Then click Add.

4 Repeat step 3 to add another field, or click Done to close the Insert Field dialog box.

Adding Pictures To add a picture from the **ClipArt Gallery** to your word processing document or database **form**, follow these steps:

1 Position the **insertion point** where you want the picture.

2 Choose the Insert ClipArt command.

3 When the ClipArt Gallery dialog box opens, select the picture you want and click Insert. (Or simply double-click the picture.)

> **Draw; Moving Objects and Pictures; Resizing Objects and Pictures**

Adding Records You can add a **record** to a database in either **form view** or **list view.**

Adding a Record in Form View

To add a record in form view, follow these steps:

1 Scroll to the record before which you want to add a new record.

2 Choose the Record Insert Record command.

Works presents a new blank record and renumbers all succeeding records.

continues

Adding Records *(continued)*

Adding a Record in List View

To add a record in list view, follow these steps:

1 **Right-click** the record number to the left of the row below which you want to add the new record.

2 Choose the Insert Record command from the **shortcut menu** to insert a blank record.

Address Book TaskWizard The Address Book
TaskWizard helps you create a database of names, addresses, phone numbers, and other information that you can use to print **envelopes, mailing labels,** or form letters—or just to look up addresses and phone numbers when you need them. To use this TaskWizard, do this:

1 In the **Works Task Launcher,** click the TaskWizards tab.

2 Select Address Book (in the Common Tasks category) and click OK.

3 The TaskWizard presents a series of options so you can set up your database just as you want it. When you've made your selection in each dialog box, click Next > to continue.

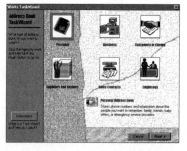

4 When you choose the last option, the TaskWizard offers to create your database. If you're satisfied with the choices you made, click Create It!

5 If you want to reconsider some of your choices, click the < Back button to back up to the previous screen. When you're ready to proceed, click Create Document. The TaskWizard creates your address book as you designed it and presents the first record for you to begin entering names and addresses.

❖ **Dialing Phone Numbers; Mail Merge**

Alignment

Alignment refers to the way Microsoft Works positions the labels and values in a spreadsheet or database. Unless you tell it otherwise, Works aligns labels and text entries to the left, and number and date entries to the right.

To change the alignment of any item, follow these steps:

1 Select the items whose alignment you want to change.

2 Choose the Format Alignment command.

3 In the Alignment tab of the Format dialog box, select the alignment options you want:

Option	What it does
General	Aligns text to the left and numbers and dates to the right
Left	Aligns the selection to the left
Right	Aligns the selection to the right
Center	Centers the selection
Fill*	Repeats the contents of a **field** or **cell** until the cell is full
Center Across Selection*	Centers the contents of the leftmost field or cell within the selected cells
Slide to Left	(**Form design view** only) Slides the selection to the left on the form when you print, eliminating blank space
Wrap Text*	Wraps the selection to the **field** or **cell** width, changing the height of its row as needed
Top*	Aligns the selection with the top of its row
Center*	Aligns the selection with the center of its row
Bottom*	Aligns the selection with the bottom of its row

*These options are not available in form design view

Different views = different alignment

The alignment you select for a field applies only to that view, allowing you to specify a different alignment in **list view**, form design view, and **report view**.

> **Column Width; Formatting; Indents and Alignment; Resizing Fields; Row Height**

A

Application Windows
An application window is a window that holds an entire application, such as Microsoft Works. An application window can contain several **document windows**.

❖ **Switching Windows**

Arguments
An argument is the information that a **function** needs to perform its task. An argument can be a **value, cell address, range** of cells, or even another function. When you insert a function, placeholders for the required arguments are shown in parentheses following the function name in the **entry bar.** For example, the SUM() function needs to know what cells to sum up. Its arguments, therefore, are cell ranges, shown in the formula bar like this: SUM(RangeRef0,RangeRef1,...). Replace each placeholder with an appropriate value or reference.

ASCII Text Files
ASCII (short for American Standard Code for Information Interchange, doo dah, doo dah) text files are files that contain only text characters, no hidden formatting codes.

ASCII files are "bare-bones," "lowest-common-denominator" files, useful for transferring information between programs or over the phone lines when the receiving program or computer cannot accept a formatted file. The information may not look pretty after you transfer it, but it usually beats retyping it when that's your only alternative.

❖ **Binary Files; Exporting Documents; Opening Documents; Saving Documents**

AutoFormat AutoFormat allows you to quickly apply presentation-quality formatting to a selected portion of a spreadsheet, or to a whole spreadsheet. To format with AutoFormat, follow these steps:

1 Select the group of **cells** you want to format.

2 Choose the Format AutoFormat command.

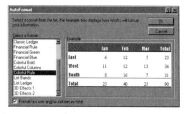

3 Select the format you want. As you select each format, the Example box shows you a sample.

4 When you've decided on a format, click OK. Works applies the format to the selected cells.

AutoSum 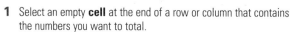 The AutoSum tool allows you to quickly total a **row** or **column** of numbers in a spreadsheet. To use the AutoSum tool, follow these steps:

1 Select an empty **cell** at the end of a row or column that contains the numbers you want to total.

2 Click the AutoSum tool. Works searches first up and then left for cells to include in the **formula**, and then proposes the cell **range** to be summed in the **entry bar**.

3 If the proposed range is correct, click the AutoSum tool again to enter the formula in the selected cell. If the range is not correct, edit the range shown in the entry bar, and then click the AutoSum tool to enter the formula in the selected cell.

Binary Files 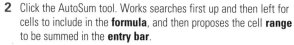 Binary files are files that contain graphics, formatting codes, or any unusual characters. Microsoft Works documents, most word processor files, and program files themselves are all examples of binary files.

ASCII Text Files; Sending and Receiving Files

Bold Characters To change characters to **bold**, select the text (or the cells that contain the text) and then press Ctrl+B or click the Bold tool.

B

Bookmarks Bookmarks allow you to quickly jump to a particular place in a document. Like a real bookmark, you can insert a Works bookmark at any place you want in a document. Then you can quickly return to that place at a later time, simply by jumping to the bookmark.

Inserting a Bookmark

To insert a bookmark, follow these steps:

1 Move the **insertion point** to where you want the bookmark.

2 Choose the Edit Bookmark command.

3 When the Bookmark Name dialog box appears, type a name for the bookmark.

4 Click OK. Works inserts a hidden bookmark with the name you typed at the insertion point.

Jumping to a Bookmark

To jump to a bookmark, follow these steps:

1 Choose the Edit Go To command, or simply press Ctrl+G.

2 When the Go To dialog box appears, type or select the name of the bookmark you want.

3 Click OK.

❖ **Go To**

Borders You can add borders around paragraphs in a word processor document, around fields or labels in a database **form**, or around **cells** and cell **ranges** in a spreadsheet.

Adding a Border

To add a border, follow these steps:

1 Select the item or items around which you want a border.

2 Choose the Format Borders And Shading command. (In the spread-sheet and database modules, choose Format Border.)

3 When the Borders And Shading dialog box appears, choose the border type, color, and line style you want.

Removing a Border

To remove a border, follow these steps:

1 Select the item or items from which you want to remove the border.

2 Choose the Format Borders And Shading command. (In the spread-sheet and database modules, choose Format Border.)

3 When the Border dialog box appears, select the empty line style (the topmost line style box).

Borders in database forms

When you add borders in a database **form**, Works adds a border around each individual label or **field** that you select. If you want a single border to surround several labels and fields, choose the Insert Rectangle command. You can then use Format Border to format the border around the rectangle. To move or resize the rectangle, see **Moving Objects and Pictures** or **Resizing Objects and Pictures**.

❖❖❖ **Page Borders; Shading**

B

Bulleted Lists You can create a bulleted list quickly by using the toolbar, or you can use the Format Paragraph command to add a bullet to paragraphs with custom indents.

Creating a Bulleted List with the Toolbar

1 Select the paragraphs you want to include in the list.

2 Click the Bullets tool.

For each paragraph, Works adds a bullet at the beginning of the paragraph and indents all the text one-quarter inch from the left **margin**.

Creating a Bulleted List with Custom Indents

1 Select the paragraphs you want to include in the list.

2 **Right-click** and choose Paragraph from the **shortcut menu.**

3 Select the Indents And Alignment tab.

4 Mark the Bulleted check box, set the indents as you want them, and then choose OK.

Works adds a bullet and an invisible tab character at the beginning of each paragraph, with left and right indents as you set them.

Using Custom Bullet Characters

"Bullets" don't have to be the ordinary • symbol; Works offers several alternatives. To select a different symbol or change its size:

1 Select the paragraphs for which you want custom bullets.

2 Right-click and choose Bullets from the shortcut menu.

3 Select the bullet and point size you want.

4 Click OK.

Removing Bullets from a Paragraph

The bullet that Works inserts is a special Works character that you cannot select or delete in the usual way. To remove a bullet:

1 Select the paragraphs you want to remove bullets from.

2 Click the Bullets tool, or choose the Format Bullets command and click Remove.

Indents and Alignment

Calculating Formulas  Works automatically calculates formulas whenever you make a change to a spreadsheet—unless you tell it not to. Why would you want to do that? One reason might be that you want to enter a series of changes and see the impact of all the changes at once. Another reason might be when you are using a very large spreadsheet and the frequent automatic recalculation is too time-consuming.

Manual Calculation

Capturing Text Works automatically captures up to 256,000 lines of text during a communications session. Works holds the text in a temporary storage area called a buffer. You can copy the buffer contents to the Clipboard and then paste them into another document. When you close the communications document, Works discards the buffer contents.

To capture incoming text directly to a file, follow these steps:

1 Choose the Tools Capture Text command, or click the Capture Text tool.

2 When the Capture Text dialog box appears, type a name for the file to hold the text.

3 Click Save.

4 When you want to stop capturing text, choose the Tools End Capture Text command, or click the Capture Text tool again.

Sending and Receiving Text Files

Cells

A cell is simply the area in a spreadsheet or in a database in **list view** where a row and a column intersect. It's in cells that you enter **values** or **formulas**.

Active Cell; Cell Address; Cell Selector

Cell Address

A cell address describes a specific location, or cell, in a spreadsheet by using the column letter and row number. For example, H17 identifies the cell at the intersection of column H and row 17.

Absolute Cell References; Mixed Cell References; Relative Cell References

Cell Selector

The cell selector is the dark outline that marks the **active cell**—the cell where the text, numbers, or formulas you type next are entered.

Changing Fonts

Works provides two ways to change **fonts**. The quick and easy way is to use the **toolbar**. But if you want to change the font's display color, or select special styles like superscript, subscript, or strikethrough, you need the deluxe tour with the Format Font And Style command.

Quick and Easy with the Toolbar

1 To change the font for text you've already typed, first select the text. To change the font for new text, place the **insertion point** where you will type the new text.

2 Click the arrow next to the toolbar's font list box and select the font you want from the list that appears.

3 If you want to change the font's **point** size, click the arrow next to the toolbar's point-size list box and select the point size you want from the list that appears.

Deluxe Tour with Format Font and Style

1 To change the font for text you've already typed, first select the text. To change the font for new text, place the insertion point where you will type the new text.

2 Choose the Format Font And Style command.

3 When the Format Font And Style dialog box appears, select the font and the options you want.

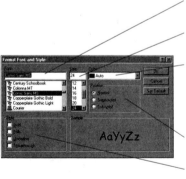

Select a font from the Font list box.

Select a point size from the Size list box.

Select a display color for the text. ("Auto" uses the color for window text set with the Windows Control Panel.)

Select a position: normal, super^{script}, or sub$_{script}$.

Select the styles you want: **bold**, *italic*, underline, ~~strikethrough~~, a ***combination***, or none.

4 When you're finished with your selections, click OK.

C

Chart Formatting

Works provides several ways to make your **charts** easier on the eyes. You can change your chart's axes, borders, colors and patterns, gridlines, and markers.

Adding or Removing a Chart Axis

To add or remove a chart's horizontal or left vertical axis, follow these steps:

1 Display the chart and choose the Format Horizontal (X) Axis command or Format Vertical (Y) Axis command.

2 When the Format Horizontal Axis or Format Vertical Axis dialog box appears, clear the No Horizontal Axis or No Vertical Axis check box to add the axis, or mark the check box to remove the axis.

3 Click OK.

To add or remove a right vertical axis, follow these steps:

1 Display the chart and choose the Format Two Vertical (Y) Axes command.

2 When the Format Two Vertical Axes dialog box appears, choose the Right radio button for at least one series to add a right axis, or choose the Left radio button for all series to remove the right axis.

3 Click OK.

Adding or Removing Chart Borders

To add a border around a chart, display the chart and choose the Format Border command. To remove the border, choose Format Border again.

Changing Chart Colors and Shading

To change the colors in a chart, follow these steps:

1 Display the chart and choose the Format Shading And Color command.

2 When the Format Shading And Color dialog box appears, select the series (or slice, for a pie chart) you want to format.

3 Select the color you want. Select Auto to have Works choose the colors for you.

4 Select the shading pattern you want. Select Auto to have Works choose the patterns for you.

5 Click Format. Or click Format All to apply your selections to all series.

6 Click Close.

C

Colors on a black-and-white printer?

No, Works can't print in color on your black-and-white printer. But it
will let you see how your color and pattern selections will appear
when printed in black and white. Choose the View Display As Printed command
after you make color and pattern choices. If you choose this command before using the Format Shading And Color command, only black-and-white color choices
appear in the Format Shading And Color dialog box. To see all the colors your
monitor can display, choose View Display As Printed again to turn off this option.

Adding or Removing Chart Gridlines

To add or remove gridlines on a chart, follow these steps:

1 Display the chart and choose the Format Horizontal (X) Axis command to add a horizontal grid, or choose the Format Vertical (Y)
Axis command to add a vertical grid.

2 When the Format Horizontal Axis or Format Vertical Axis dialog box
appears, mark the Show Gridlines check box to add gridlines, or
clear the check box to remove gridlines.

3 Click OK.

Changing Chart Markers

To change the markers on a line, stacked line, x-y scatter, combination,
or radar chart, follow these steps:

1 Display the chart and choose Format Shading And Color.

2 When the Format Shading And Color dialog box appears, select the
series whose markers you want to change.

3 Select the marker shape you want in the Markers box. Select Auto
to have Works choose the marker shape for you. Select None to remove markers for the selected series.

4 Click Format to change the markers for the selected series, or click
Format All to format all series with the selected marker.

5 Click Close.

Charts With Works, you can create many different kinds of charts by using the data in a spreadsheet. You can save and print the chart by itself, or you can insert it into a word processing document or database **form**.

Creating a Chart

1 Open the spreadsheet containing the data you want to chart, or open a new spreadsheet document and enter the values to be charted.

2 Select the values you want to chart.

3 Choose the Tools Create New Chart command or click the New Chart tool.

4 When the New Chart dialog box appears, choose how you want your chart to look. As you make your selections, the sample chart in the dialog box changes to show how the chart will look with your data.

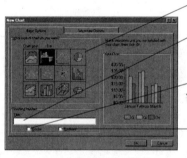

Click the type of chart you want.

Type a title for your chart (if you want one) in the Title box.

Mark the Border check box to add a border around the chart.

Mark the Gridlines check box to show gridlines on the chart.

5 On the Advanced Options tab, answer the three questions about your data by selecting the appropriate radio buttons:

1) Select Across to chart each spreadsheet *row* as a separate group, or choose Down to chart each spreadsheet *column* as a separate group.

2) Select Legend Text if the first item in each data group is a description of the group, or select A Category if the first item is a value to be charted.

3) Select Category Labels if the first data group contains labels for the x-axis, or select A Value (Y) Series if the first group contains values to be charted.

6 When you're satisfied with the way the sample chart looks, click OK.

What's a series?

A series is simply chart-talk for a group of values that you want to chart. Pie charts have just one series—whatever you are charting. Other chart types have two or more series. For example, if you are charting your waistline for the last 12 months (not a good application for a pie chart!), your chart has two series—the months, which run along the horizontal x-axis (called an x-series or category series), and your measurements, which are plotted using the vertical y-axis (called a y-series or value series).

Creating a Chart in a Word Processing Document or Database Form

To create a chart from within a word processing document or database form, follow these steps:

1 Choose the Insert Chart command.

2 When the Insert Chart dialog box appears, select Create A New Chart and click OK.

3 Works displays a reminder telling you to enter the values to be charted in the spreadsheet. Click OK.

4 Works embeds an empty spreadsheet directly in your document. Enter the values you want to chart.

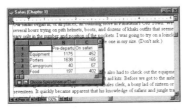

5 Select the values in the spreadsheet you want to chart.

6 Click the Chart button in the lower left corner of the spreadsheet.

7 Works displays the New Chart dialog box. Follow the steps above under "Creating a Chart" to select the chart options you want.

8 Click OK. Works displays the chart. To continue working on your word processing document or database form, click anywhere outside the chart.

To change the values the chart is based on, double-click the chart in your document or form and then click the Spreadsheet button at the bottom of the chart pane. When the spreadsheet appears, make the changes you want and click the Chart button. Click outside the chart to return to your document or form.

continues

Charts *(continued)*

Name that chart

Works saves up to eight charts with each spreadsheet automatically. But it gives them mundane names like Chart1, Chart2, and so on. To name your chart so you can find it more easily, choose the Tools Rename Chart command. In the Rename Chart dialog box, highlight your chart, type a name in the name box, and click Rename.

Adding an Existing Chart to a Word Processing Document or to a Database Form

When you add a chart to a word processing document or to a database form, the chart automatically updates whenever the spreadsheet it is based on changes.

To add a chart, follow these steps:

1 Open the spreadsheet that contains the chart you want to add.

2 Open the word processing document or database form that you want to add the chart to.

3 Choose Insert Chart.

4 In the Insert Chart dialog box, select Use An Existing Chart.

5 Select a spreadsheet from the list of spreadsheets.

6 Select a chart.

7 Click OK.

To link or not to link

Linking is a powerful feature that keeps imported charts in sync with their roots. But you might not want the chart you inserted to change every time the original spreadsheet changes. In that case, choose the Edit Links command, select the name of the chart, and select the Manual radio button.

Chart Formatting; Chart Text; Chart Types; OLE Linking and Embedding

Chart Text

Most charts are more useful if you add some text to identify their different parts. Works does not allow you to add text to a chart by typing directly on the chart. But you can add titles, a legend, labels for the horizontal axis (category labels), and labels for each plotted value (data labels).

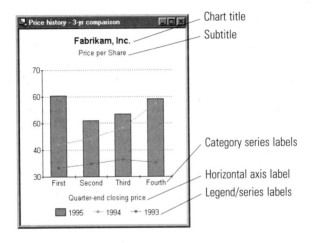

Chart title
Subtitle

Category series labels

Horizontal axis label
Legend/series labels

Chart Titles

Chart titles identify the chart itself and its key elements. You can add a main chart title, a subtitle, and titles for the vertical and horizontal axes. To add a title, follow these steps:

1 With the chart displayed, choose the Edit Titles command.

2 When the Edit Titles dialog box appears, type the title you want (or a reference to a spreadsheet cell containing the title) in the appropriate box.

3 Click OK.

To change or delete a title, follow the same steps and make the changes or deletions you want in the Edit Titles dialog box.

continues

Chart Text *(continued)*

Chart Legends

A chart legend is a set of labels that identify the series of values plotted in the chart. When you create an area, bar, or line chart, Works automatically adds a legend for you at the bottom of the chart. If the spreadsheet rows or columns that the chart is based on include titles, Works uses those titles for the legend. Otherwise, Works supplies the series labels Series 1, Series 2, and so on.

To add a chart legend, follow these steps:

1   With the chart displayed, choose the Edit Legend/Series Labels command.

2   When the Edit Legend/Series Label dialog box appears, make sure the Auto Series Labels check box is not marked. If it is marked, Works uses its built-in Series 1, Series 2 labels.

3   Type the name you want (or a reference to a spreadsheet cell containing the name) for each series in your chart.

4   If the chart is an area chart, and you want the series labels inside the charted areas rather than as a legend at the bottom of the chart, select Use As Area Labels.

5   Click OK.

To change or delete a legend, follow the same steps and make the changes or deletions you want in the Edit Legend/Series Label dialog box.

Chart Labels for Pie Charts

Pie chart slices can have two labels each. For each label, you can select from five different label types:

Label type	What it shows
Values	The values used to plot the slices
Percentages	The percentage of the total each slice represents
Cell Contents	The contents of any cell range you specify
1, 2, 3, ...	Sequential numbers for each slice
None	No label

To add labels to a pie chart, follow these steps:

1 With the pie chart displayed, choose the Edit Data Labels command.

2 When the Format Data Labels dialog box appears, choose the labels you want. If you choose Cell Contents, enter the spreadsheet cell range containing the labels you want in the Cell Range box.

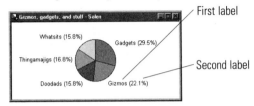

First label

Second label

3 Click OK.

To change labels for a pie chart, follow the same steps and make the changes you want in the Format Data Labels dialog box. To delete labels completely, select the None option for both labels.

Chart Labels for Other Charts

To add labels to area, bar, line, or radar charts, you enter the labels into the spreadsheet the chart is based on, and then copy and paste them into place in the chart. You can paste the labels along the horizontal axis (called category labels), or you can paste the labels into the body of the chart (called value or data labels).

To add labels to a chart other than a pie chart, follow these steps:

1 In the spreadsheet the chart is based on, enter the text or numbers you want for the labels. (To access the spreadsheet for a chart embedded in another document, double-click the chart and then choose View Spreadsheet.)

2 Select the cells containing the label text or numbers.

3 Choose the Edit Copy command.

4 Choose the View Chart command to switch to the chart you want to label.

5 Choose the Edit Series command.

continues

Chart Text *(continued)*

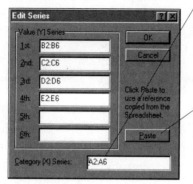

6 When the Edit Series dialog box appears, move the insertion point to the Category (X) Series box to add the labels to the horizontal axis.

7 Click the Paste button.

8 Click OK.

To change labels, follow the same steps and paste the new labels in the Edit Series dialog box. To delete labels, choose Edit Series and make the deletions you want in the Edit Series dialog box.

Chart Types

Works provides 12 different types of charts for you to choose from: area charts, bar charts, line charts, pie charts, stacked line charts, x-y scatter charts, radar charts, combination charts, 3-D area charts, 3-D bar charts, 3-D line charts, and 3-D pie charts. Works shows an example of each chart type when you create a new chart, or when you change the type for an existing chart.

Choosing a Chart Type for a New Chart

When you create a chart, Works presents an icon for each chart type in its New Chart dialog box.

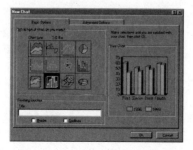

You can see what your data will look like in each chart type by selecting different types in the New Chart dialog box. Each time you select a chart type, Works shows you a sample chart using your data.

Changing the Chart Type for an Existing Chart

To change the type for an existing chart, follow these steps:

1 Open the spreadsheet that the chart is based on. (To change the type for a chart embedded in another document, double-click the chart and skip to step 4.)

2 Choose the View Chart command.

3 When the Charts dialog box appears, select the chart you want to change and click OK.

4 Choose the Format Chart Type command and then select the type of chart you want.

5 Click the Variations tab and select the chart that includes the options you want.

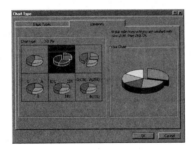

Circular Reference

See *Reference, Circular.* (Just kidding!) If you see the message CIRC in the **status bar** when entering **formulas** in a spreadsheet, you've fallen into the circular reference trap: The formula in one cell uses a **value** in a second cell, but the formula in the second cell uses a value from the first cell—something like, cell B1 contains =10*C1, and cell C1 contains =10*B1. To get out of the trap, simply change one of the formulas.

Dependents; Precedents

ClipArt Gallery 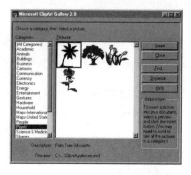 Works comes with a collection of pictures, or clip art, you can insert into your word processing documents and database **forms**.

Viewing the ClipArt Gallery

To see the pictures in the gallery, choose the Insert ClipArt command.

The ClipArt Gallery organizes the available pictures into categories as shown in the list box at the left side of the dialog box. You can select the category you want to see or you can select All Categories to view all pictures.

Maintaining the ClipArt Gallery

You can do several things to keep the ClipArt Gallery organized and up-to-date. To use the gallery maintenance options, click the Organize button in the ClipArt Gallery dialog box.

C

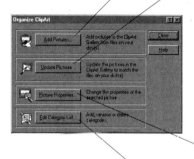

Click Add Pictures to add a specific picture or collection to the ClipArt Gallery.

Click Update Pictures to update the ClipArt Gallery to reflect any additions, changes, or deletions you made to pictures stored on your computer. Choose Refresh also to locate pictures on your computer that you might want to add to the gallcry.

Click Picture Properties to move a picture from one category to another, or to change the description of the image.

Click Edit Category List to change the name of a category, or to delete a category.

 Adding Pictures

Clipboard 📄🗂️🖨️🗂️ The Clipboard is a temporary holding area. It is a feature in Windows that lets you move information between one part of a document and another part, between one Works document and another, or between Works and another Windows-based program. You use the Clipboard whenever you use the Edit Cut or Edit Copy commands. Works stores the text or picture you cut or copy on the Clipboard temporarily until you decide to insert it somewhere with the Edit Paste command.

continues

Clipboard *(continued)*

Two important things to remember about the Clipboard:

• It holds only one item at a time. Each time you use Edit Cut or Edit Copy to put something on the Clipboard, you replace whatever was previously on the Clipboard.

• It is temporary. When you turn off your computer or exit Windows, the contents of the Clipboard are lost.

⁘ **OLE Linking and Embedding**

Closing Documents

To close a Works document, click the Close button—the one that looks like an X in the document window's upper right corner—or choose the File Close command. If you've made changes to the document since you last saved it, Works asks if you want to save the document.

Color

You can change the color of most parts of Works documents.

Coloring database forms ⁘ **Shading**
Coloring spreadsheet cells ⁘ **Shading**
Coloring text ⁘ **Changing Fonts**
Coloring borders ⁘ **Borders**
Changing chart colors ⁘ **Chart Formatting**

Columns

In a spreadsheet each column (a single vertical line of **cells**) is identified by a letter, which appears at the top of the column. In **list view**, every database **field** occupies a column. You can apply anything you know about spreadsheet columns (such as how to adjust the **column width** or select columns) to fields.

⁘ **Inserting Columns and Rows; Selecting Columns and Rows; Text Columns**

Column Width You can use the mouse or the Format Column Width command to change a column's width.

Drag the edge of the column letter to change the width of that column.

The perfect column width

To adjust the column width to fit the widest entry in the column, double-click the column letter or click the Best Fit button in the Column Width dialog box.

Communication Settings Before you can communicate with another computer, you need to tell Works how to talk to the other computer. You do so by choosing the Settings Communication command.

Works is pretty good at detecting your computer's needs, so you most likely will not have to change these settings.

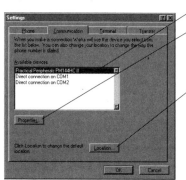

Select your modem.

Click Properties to select a port, set the number of data bits, and other technical stuff.

Click Location if you move your computer to a different area code or to a location that has call waiting or special dialing requirements.

continues

41

Communication Settings *(continued)*

Selecting common settings

Windows has probably already configured your modem properly to
work with most BBS's and online services. The only change you're
likely to need is to switch between *8,n,1* (data bits, parity, stop bits)
and *7,e,1*. You'll find buttons on the toolbar to make this switch with a single
click.

 Phone Settings; Protocol; Terminal Settings

Control-Menu Commands The Control
menu is the menu that appears when you click the small
icon in the upper left corner of a window. It contains a
number of handy commands that let you manipulate
Works windows.

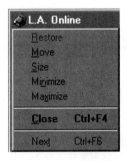

Copying The easiest way to copy text, pictures,
charts, cells, or **ranges** in Works is with **drag and drop.**

Copying from One Window to Another

Using drag and drop, you can copy information to another similar
Works document, a different kind of Works document, or to any
document created in a Windows-based application.

1 Open both documents and arrange them so you can see them both.

2 Select the information you want to copy and drag it to the other
window.

Copying Within the Same Window

To copy information from one place to another within the same
document, hold down Ctrl while you drag. Otherwise, Works thinks you
want to move the selection and cuts the information from its old
location.

⁝ Clipboard

Copying Data  You can copy data within a **database** the
same way you copy text in a word processor document:
You hold down Ctrl as you **drag and drop**, or use Edit
Copy and Edit Paste.

But did you know you can copy data from a database to
another Works database, a Works spreadsheet, or a
Works word processor document? You use the same
technique:

1 Open the source and destination documents and arrange the windows so both are visible.

2 Select the data you want to copy.

3 Point to the border of the selected data, and then drag it to the
other window.

When you drag database information to a word processor
document, each **field** is separated by a tab character, and
each **record** ends with a paragraph mark.

When you drag data to a spreadsheet, each field becomes
a **column** and each record becomes a **row**; the
spreadsheet looks much like database **list view**.

You can also drag information to many other Windows-
based applications. Which ones? Try it!

⁝ Nonprinting Characters

C

Copying Formatting
To copy just the style or format of text without copying the text itself, follow these steps:

1 Select the text whose style or format you want.
2 Choose the Edit Copy command.
3 Select the character or paragraph you want to copy the formatting to.
4 Choose the Edit Paste Special command.
5 In the Paste Special dialog box, select Character Style or Paragraph Format.
6 Click OK.

Copying Formulas
To copy **formulas** (or any other cell contents) in a spreadsheet, follow these steps:

1 Select the cells containing the formulas you want to copy.
2 Point to the border of the selected cells, and then drag the selection to another window. Or, to copy the selected cells to another location within the same spreadsheet, hold down Ctrl and drag the selection.

Copying Values; Filling Cells

Copying Objects and Pictures
You can copy objects (such as **Note-It** notes, **tables,** and **charts**) and pictures within a document by selecting the object, holding down Ctrl, and dragging the object where you want it.

Alternatively, you can use the Edit Copy and Edit Paste commands.

Drag and Drop; Moving Objects and Pictures; Selecting Objects

Copying Text
The easiest way to copy selected text is to hold down Ctrl and drag the text to the desired location.

C

You can also copy text by following these steps:

1 Select the text you want to copy.

2 Choose the Edit Copy command, which places a copy of the text on the **Clipboard**.

3 Place the **insertion point** where you want the text.

4 Choose the Edit Paste command.

Drag and Drop; Moving Text; Selecting Text

Copying Values
To copy **values** without copying the actual **formulas** that produce the values, follow these steps:

1 Select the cell or range that contains the formulas.

2 Choose the Edit Copy command.

3 Move the **cell selector** where you want to insert the values.

4 Choose the Edit Paste Special command.

5 When the Paste Special dialog box appears, select the Values Only radio button.

6 Click OK.

Copying Formulas

Counting Words
To count the number of words in a document, choose the Tools Word Count command. To count the words in a portion of a document, select the portion you want to count before choosing the Tools Word Count command.

Currency Symbols
Works uses a currency symbol, usually a dollar sign, for **values** you format as currency. But if you're the worldly type, you might want Works to use a different currency symbol, like £ or ¥. To change the currency symbol, follow these steps:

1 Click the Start button, choose Settings, and choose Control Panel.

2 Double-click the Regional Settings icon.

3 Click the Currency tab.

continues

C

Currency Symbols *(continued)*

4 Enter the currency symbol you want in the Currency Symbol text box. (If the symbol isn't on your keyboard, use Character Map to enter it.)

5 Click OK. Your new settings take effect immediately.

:: **Formatting Numbers; Symbols**

Customizing Toolbars 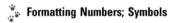 Each Works module has its own **toolbar**, and you can customize each toolbar to fit the way you work by adding special tools you use and by removing standard tools you don't use.

To customize a toolbar, choose the Tools Customize Toolbar command or double-click any blank space on the toolbar to open the Customize Works Toolbar dialog box.

To remove a tool from the toolbar, drag the tool anywhere off the toolbar.

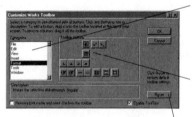 To add a tool to the toolbar, select the category of the tool you want to add from the list in the Categories box.

Then drag the tool you want to add to its new location on the toolbar.

To move a tool to a different position on the toolbar, drag the tool to its new location.

 To reset the toolbar to its original configuration, click the Reset button.

When you've got the toolbar the way you want it, click OK.

 Quick Reference contains a complete list of available toolbar buttons.

Cutting

When you cut information, you remove it from its place in your document, spreadsheet, or database form and place it temporarily on the **Clipboard**—usually in preparation to move it somewhere else by **pasting** it.

To cut information, select it and then choose the Edit Cut command, **right-click** and choose Cut, press Ctrl+X, or click the Cut tool.

Databases

A database is a Works document you use to organize and access information. What kinds of information? Your address book; a mailing list; recipes; business contact list; a home inventory; an audio, video, or book collection—in short, anything you might keep track of with a Rolodex or index cards—is a great candidate for a database.

Creating Databases

The easiest way to create a database is to use a **TaskWizard**.

1 Choose the File New command to open the **Works Task Launcher**.

2 Select an application closest to what you want from the TaskWizards list. (You can customize the database after the TaskWizard creates it.)

3 Click OK.

Fields; Records

Date and Time Functions

Works has nine **functions** that make working with dates and times in spreadsheets and databases easier. For example, you can use the DAY(), MONTH(), or YEAR() function to extract the day of the month, the month, or the year from a particular date. An especially handy date function is the NOW() function. Put this **formula** in your spreadsheet, and it will always display the correct current date:

=NOW()

Date Formats

Works gives you several different ways to format dates in your spreadsheets and databases. To set or change a date format, select the **cell** or **field** containing the date, and then choose the Format Number or Format Field command. Select the Date radio button and select the format you want from the list.

Formatting Numbers

Default Address Book

Although you can store and use as many address books and **databases** as you want, Works lets you designate one as your default address book. It proposes to use the default address book whenever you print **envelopes** or **mailing labels**, and you can quickly open it from any Works module by choosing the Tools Address Book command.

You can select a database to be the default by choosing Tools Options and clicking the Address Book tab.

Address Book TaskWizard

Deleting Columns and Rows

To delete or remove columns or rows from a spreadsheet, select the columns or rows, **right-click**, and then choose the Delete Row or Delete Column command from the **shortcut menu**.

To delete or clear column or row contents without removing the column or row itself, select the column or row and then press the Del key.

Erasing Cells

Deleting Fields

To delete or remove fields from a database, select the fields and then choose the Edit Delete Selection command in **form design view**, or the Record Delete Field command in **list view**.

To delete or clear field contents without removing the field itself, select the field and choose Edit Clear.

D

Deleting Files

Works saves all of your documents and forms on disk as files. To delete a file, choose the File Open command. **Right-click** the name of the document you want to delete, and choose Delete from the **shortcut menu**.

Deleting Objects

To delete objects (such as pictures, **Note-It** notes, **tables**, and **charts**), click the object to select it and press the Del key.

Deleting Records

To delete a record in **list view**, **right-click** the record and choose Delete Record from the **shortcut menu**. To delete a record in **form view**, display the record and choose the Record Delete Record command.

*** Hiding Records

Deleting Text

To delete text, select the text and press the Del key.

Dependents

A dependent **cell** is one containing a **formula** that references another cell. For example, if cell A5 contains the formula =A3+A4, then cell A5 is dependent; it depends on obtaining values from cells A3 and A4 before it can calculate properly.

*** ERR Message; Precedents

Dialing Phone Numbers If you have a modem
connected to your computer and a telephone connected
to the modem, you can use Works to dial the phone for
you. Simply select the number you want to dial in a word
processor document, database, or spreadsheet, and then
choose the Tools Dial This Number command. Your modem dials the number, and then you can pick up the telephone handset.

Easy Connect

Dialog Boxes   A dialog box is a mini-window
that Works displays when it needs some information
from you. A typical dialog box has several options for you
to choose.

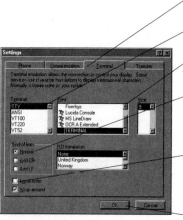

Click a tab to view a "page" of options.

Select an item from a list.

Click the arrows to scroll the list.

Click a radio button to choose an option. Click another button to choose a different option.

Mark one or more check boxes to select options. Clear its check box to turn an option off.

Click OK when you're satisfied with your selections.

Need some help?

If you don't understand what a dialog box option does, click the ques-
tion-mark button in the upper right corner of the dialog box and then
click the option you're unsure about. A small window pops up to explain the option.

Documents

A Works document is what you see when you open a file. It can be a word processor document, a spreadsheet document, a database document, or a communications document. You can open as many as eight documents at one time, each within its own window.

Document Windows

A document window is a window that holds an open **document**. Just as an **application window** is fully contained within your computer's display screen, a document window is fully contained within its application window. You can have up to eight document windows open at a time in Works.

Control-Menu Commands

Drag and Drop

Drag and drop is a technique that lets you move or copy parts of a document using the mouse.

Moving with Drag and Drop

To move part of a document, select it and then drag it to its new location. (By drag, I mean click the mouse button and hold it down while you move the mouse pointer to the destination. The "drop" part comes in when you let go of the button.) To drag cells in a spreadsheet or in database list view, you must point to the selected cells' border before you click.

Copying with Drag and Drop

The technique for copying part of another document is exactly the same as for moving (described above), except you hold down the Ctrl key while you drag.

Draw

Draw is the Microsoft tool that lets you create or modify drawings that you can insert into a word processor document or database **form**.

continues

Draw *(continued)*

Creating or Changing a Drawing

To create a drawing, choose the Insert Drawing command. To change a drawing, double-click the drawing. When the Draw window appears, choose the tool you need from the Draw toolbar.

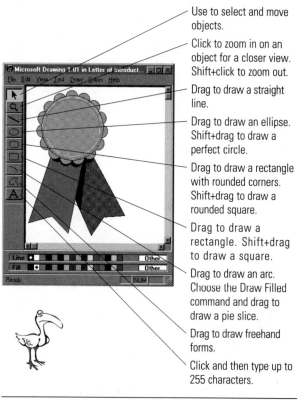

Use to select and move objects.

Click to zoom in on an object for a closer view. Shift+click to zoom out.

Drag to draw a straight line.

Drag to draw an ellipse. Shift+drag to draw a perfect circle.

Drag to draw a rectangle with rounded corners. Shift+drag to draw a rounded square.

Drag to draw a rectangle. Shift+drag to draw a square.

Drag to draw an arc. Choose the Draw Filled command and drag to draw a pie slice.

Drag to draw freehand forms.

Click and then type up to 255 characters.

Adding a Drawing to a Document

To add a drawing you create with Microsoft Draw to your word processing or database document, follow these steps:

1 From the Microsoft Draw window, choose the File Exit And Return command.

2 Works asks if you want to update the document. Choose Yes to return to Works and add the drawing.

3 Works inserts the drawing at the insertion point.

E

Easy Calc Easy Calc is a tool that makes it easy to enter simple **formulas** and use **functions** by pointing and clicking. Start by clicking the Easy Calc tool, and then click the button for the type of calculation you want to make. Follow the on-screen instructions, which direct you to point at the **cells** that contain the data on which you'll base your calculations and then point at the cell where you want the result.

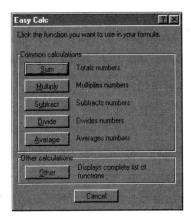

Easy Connect The Easy Connect dialog box lists the communication connections you have set up, and lets you easily reconnect to one of them or define a new connection. The Easy Connect dialog box appears when you click the Communications button in the **Works Task Launcher** or, more simply, when you choose the Phone Easy Connect command while a communications document is already open and active.

continues

Easy Connect *(continued)*

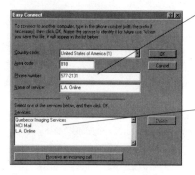

Type the phone number and the name of the service to connect to the service for the first time.

Or select the name of a service from the list to reestablish a previous connection.

❖ **New Documents; Phone Settings; Communication Settings; Modem Setup**

Easy Formats

Easy Formats allow you to apply consistent styles to various elements in your word processor documents. Works comes with predefined Easy Formats for various headings, lists, indented paragraphs, and so on. You can apply any of those styles or create your own.

Applying an Existing Easy Format

1 Select the paragraphs that you want to format.

2 Click the Easy Formats tool and select the style you want from the menu that appears. If the style you want is not listed, choose More Easy Formats.

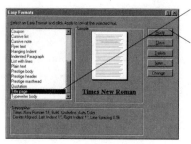

3 Select the Easy Format you want.

4 Click Apply.

E

Creating New Easy Formats

The easiest way to create a new style is to use a paragraph that's formatted just the way you want it. Follow these steps:

1 Select a paragraph in your document.

2 Visit each of the commands on the Format menu—Font And Style, Paragraph, Tabs, Borders And Shading, and Bullets—to set up your example paragraph.

3 Click the Easy Formats tool and choose Create From Selection.

4 Type a name for your selection.

5 Click Done.

Modifying Existing Styles

1 Choose the Format Easy Formats command.

2 Select the name of the style you want to change.

3 Click Change.

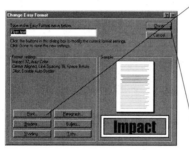

4 Click the button for the formatting you want to change—Font, Paragraph, Borders, Bullets, Shading, or Tabs—and make your changes.

5 Click Done to close the Change Easy Format dialog box.

6 Click Close to close the Easy Formats dialog box.

∴ **Bulleted Lists; Borders; Fonts; Indents and Alignment; Line Spacing; Shading; Tabs**

Easy Text

Easy Text lets you enter any amount of text simply by typing its Easy Text name (an abbreviation you define) and pressing F3. It's useful for entry of "boilerplate" text, closing paragraphs to a letter, and other text that you use repeatedly.

Defining Easy Text

1 Type the text you want to save as an Easy Text entry.

2 Select the text.

3 Choose the Insert Easy Text New Easy Text command.

4 Type a name for your Easy Text. (This is the name you'll type whenever you want to enter your Easy Text.)

5 If you want to apply an **Easy Format** to your text, click Format. Then select an Easy Format and click Apply.

6 Click Done.

Easy formatting for your Easy Text

By default, your Easy Text entries retain whatever Easy Format you apply when you define them. If you don't want to include formatting information, choose Insert Easy Texts More Easy Texts. Select the Easy Text you want, clear the Insert With Formatting check box, and click Insert.

Editing Cells

To replace the contents of a **cell**, select the cell and begin typing. Notice that as you type, your new entry appears in two places: in the **active cell** and in the **entry bar**. If you want to move the **insertion point** within your new entry—or if you want to make minor changes to an existing entry—press F2 or click in the entry bar where you want the insertion point.

When the entry bar contains the text, **value**, or **formula** that you want to appear in the cell, press Enter or click the entry bar's check-mark button. If you change your mind and decide not to change the cell's contents, press Esc or click the entry bar's × button.

E

Faster editing of multiple cells

If you are going to make entries in several cells, select them all before you begin making entries. When multiple cells are selected, Works automatically makes the next cell in the selection the active cell when you press Enter or click the check-mark button.

 Erasing Cells; Functions; Selecting Cells

Editing Charts  To change a **chart** that you've al-
ready created, begin by double-clicking the chart. (In the spreadsheet module, choose the View Chart command.) The menus change to indicate that the charting module is active. You can then change the **chart type**, add or delete chart titles, edit the data in the chart—in fact, do anything you can when you create a new chart.

Chart Formatting

Editing Records You can edit **records** in a **database** in ei-
ther **form view** or **list view**. The procedure for editing data items is exactly the same as the procedure for **editing cells**.

Adding Records; Deleting Records

Editing Text To edit text that you've already entered,
select the text that you want to change. Then type; the new text you type replaces the selection. If you want to add new text without replacing existing text, position the **insertion point** and begin typing.

Entering Text; Selecting Text

E

Embedding and Linking Existing Objects

To create an object from an existing file (a Works document or a file from another application), follow these steps:

1 Place the **insertion point** where you want the object.

2 Choose the Insert Object command.

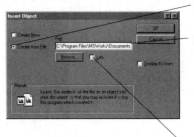

3 Select the Create From File radio button.

4 Type the name of the file in the File text box. If you're not sure of the name—or you're a lousy typist—choose the Browse button and select the filename from the list that appears.

5 If you want to link the object (so that any time you make a change in the original file, your Works document gets updated), mark the Link check box.

6 Click OK.

 The easiest way

To insert a **range** or **chart** from an open Works spreadsheet into a word processor document or database **form**, choose the Insert Spreadsheet or Insert Chart command. Works displays a dialog box that lists the open spreadsheets and their named ranges or charts; simply select the one you want to insert.

Drag and Drop; OLE Linking and Embedding

Embedding New Objects

To create a new object from an application other than Microsoft Works and embed it in a Works word processor document or database **form** (you must be in **form design view**), follow these steps:

1 Place the **insertion point** where you want the object.

2 Choose the Insert Object command.

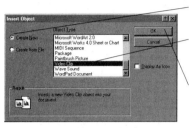

3 Select the Create New radio button.

4 Select the type of object you want to embed.

5 Click OK. Works starts the application associated with the object type, allowing you to create the object.

OLE Linking and Embedding

Ending Lines Thanks to **word wrap,** you normally don't have to worry about line endings; they just happen. If you want to end a line without ending a **paragraph**, press Shift+Enter.

Endnotes Endnotes, like **footnotes**, are used for documenting quotations or for making incidental comments that you don't want to include in the main text. Endnotes, however, appear at the end of the document instead of at the bottom of the page where the reference occurs. If that's what you want, follow these steps:

1 Create your footnotes in the usual way. (See **Footnotes**.)

2 Choose File Page Setup and select the Other Options tab.

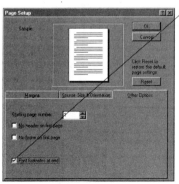

3 Mark the Print Footnotes At End check box.

Entering Data

You can enter data—text, numbers, or **formulas**—into a database in either **list view** or **form view**.

Entering Text or Numbers

Select the **field** where you want to enter data and then type. Press Tab to move to the next field. Pressing Tab in the last field of a **record** moves the highlight to the first field of the next record.

Entering Formulas

You enter formulas just like text or numbers—except you must begin the entry with an equal sign (=). To calculate the selling price for an inventory item in a field, for example, you might enter this formula:

=Cost*1.5

Works displays the formula in the **entry bar** and the result of the formula in the field. Works automatically enters the formula in every record in the database.

Proposing default entries

Works can automatically enter information that is the same for most records in a database. To set a default value, select the field and choose Format Field (list view and **form design view** only). Mark the Automatically Enter A Default Value check box and type the value you want. For example, if most members of your photography club live in California, make CA the default value for the State field. Works proposes CA as the entry for each new record. But if you have a member who moved to Nevada (probably to avoid taxes), just type *NV* when you enter her record.

Entering Numbers

To enter information such as numeric **values, formulas**, or labels in a spreadsheet, click the **cell** where you want the information and then type.

⁙ **Filling Cells; Fill Series; Formula Bar**

Entering Text

To enter text in a word processor document, just type away. Were you expecting this to be difficult?

Don't press Enter (except at the end of a paragraph)

When you reach the right margin, keep typing. (Don't press Enter.) Works moves the **insertion point** to the next line automatically. This feature is called **word wrap**, and you'll really come to appreciate it if you later make changes to your text, because the line endings will automatically change as needed.

Entering Text on a Database Form

Follow these steps to place text anywhere on a database **form**:

1 Choose the View Form Design command.

2 Place the **insertion point** where you want to add text.

3 Type your text and press Enter when you're done. (Don't end your text with a colon, because then the text becomes the name of a new field. If that's what you want, see **Adding Fields**.)

Ending Lines; Entering Data

Entry Bar

The entry bar is the area beneath the **toolbar**, and it's the place where you enter **values** and **formulas** into **cells** or **fields**.

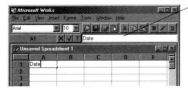

The entry bar displays the contents of the **active cell**. If you click the formula or press F2, you can edit the cell's contents.

Envelopes

You can create envelopes from within a word processor or database document by choosing the Tools Envelopes command. (If you choose this command from a word processor document, Works adds an envelope to the open document. If you choose Tools Envelopes from the database module or if you run the Envelopes **TaskWizard** from the **Works Task Launcher**, Works automatically opens a word processor document, which is where you'll actually create the envelopes.)

continues

Envelopes *(continued)*

Creating an Envelope

1 Choose the Tools Envelopes command or select the Envelopes TaskWizard.

2 Works displays a page of instructions. After you review the instructions, click Next and Works leads you through the process of filling out the necessary information. Click Next after you complete each tab.

3 Select an envelope size on the Envelope Size tab.

4 If you want to create envelopes from database records, select the database on the Database tab. Skip to step 6 if you're printing a single envelope.

5 On the Recipients tab, specify the database records for which you want to print envelopes.

6 On the Return Address tab, type the information that you want in the envelope's upper left corner.

7 On the Main Address tab, select each field you want and click Add Field. Click New Line to insert a line break. If you're printing a single envelope, simply type the delivery address in the Main Address box.

8 To print your envelopes immediately, select the number of copies you want and click Print when you reach the Printing tab. Or click Close to create a document, which you can format and edit before printing.

Select the address first

Select the text that you want in the Address text box before you choose the Tools Envelopes command, and Works automatically inserts it for you on the Main Address tab.

 Mail Merge; Options

Erasing

You can erase (or delete) cells, columns, rows, fields, records, text, objects, and files.

Clearing cell contents **Erasing Cells**
Removing columns **Deleting Columns and Rows**
Removing fields **Deleting Fields**
Removing files **Deleting Files**
Removing objects **Deleting Objects**
Removing records **Deleting Records**
Removing rows **Deleting Columns and Rows**
Removing text **Deleting Text**

Erasing Cells

You can erase the contents of one or more **cells**. To do so, select the cells you want to erase and then choose the Edit Clear command or, more simply, press Del.

Erasing a cell does not remove the cell from the spreadsheet or database; it simply clears the cell's contents.

Clearing a formula in a database

Database fields that contain a **formula** act a little differently from other cells. If you want to erase a formula in **list view**, you must select the entire field and then choose the Edit Clear Formula command.

 **Deleting Columns and Rows; Deleting Fields; Deleting Records; Selecting Cells**

ERR Message  If you see a **cell** that contains "ERR," that cell's **formula** has an err. Er, I mean error. This occurs when your formula attempts a mathematically impossible feat, such as dividing by zero or calculating the square root of a negative number.

Cells that are **dependent** on an ERR cell also contain ERR.

To ERR is human

Sometimes you'll *want* the ERR message to appear as a signal that there's an error somewhere in your data. That's easy: Use the ERR() **function**. The following example displays ERR if the value of cell A5 is less than 10; otherwise it displays the value of cell A5:

=IF(A5<10,ERR(),A5)

∴ **Informational Functions**

Exiting Works To exit from Works—or almost any other Windows-based application—you can use any of these techniques:

- Choose the File Exit Works command
- Press Alt+F4
- Double-click the Control-menu icon
- Click the Exit Works button in the **Works Task Launcher**

If you have any open documents that you haven't saved, Works asks if you want to save them before quitting.

∴ **Closing Documents; Control-Menu Commands; Saving Documents**

Exporting Documents 🖊️🖊️🖊️🖊️ Exporting is the process of saving a file in a format that you can use with another program. You might find this ability useful if you use Works on a portable computer and Microsoft Word and Excel on your desktop computer, for example.

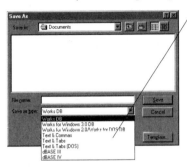

To export a document, choose the File Save As command, and then select a format that your other program can open.

You can export this file type	From these modules
Comma-separated text	🖊️🖊️
dBASE III	🖊️
dBASE IV	🖊️
Lotus 1-2-3 version 2.*x*	🖊️
Microsoft Excel versions 4.0, 5.0, and 7.0	🖊️
Microsoft Windows Write	🖊️
Microsoft Word for Macintosh version 6.0	🖊️
Microsoft Word for MS-DOS versions 3.0–6.0	🖊️
Microsoft Word for Windows versions 2.0, 6.0, and 7.0	🖊️
Microsoft Works for Macintosh versions 3.0 and 4.0	🖊️🖊️🖊️
Microsoft Works for MS-DOS	🖊️🖊️🖊️
Microsoft Works for Windows versions 2.0 and 3.0	🖊️🖊️🖊️
Rich text format	🖊️
Tab-separated text	🖊️🖊️
Text	🖊️ 🖊️
WordPerfect versions 5.*x*, 6.0, and 6.1	🖊️

continues

Exporting Documents *(continued)*

Works can also import (open) files saved in each of these formats; see **Opening Documents**.

☀ **ASCII Text Files; Lotus 1-2-3; Microsoft Excel; Microsoft Word; Sharing Works Data; WordPerfect; Write**

Field Lines Field lines are the dotted lines that indicate the **field** locations in the database **form view**. You can make them appear and disappear by switching to **form design view** and then choosing the View Field Lines command.

Printing field lines

The setting of the View Field Lines command does not control whether field lines print when you print a form. To control that feature, choose the File Page Setup command, select the Other Options tab, and use the Print Field Lines check box.

Field Names Every **field** in a **database** must have a name by which you can identify it. Works imposes only a couple of restrictions in naming a field: The name cannot be longer than 15 characters, and it can't start with an apostrophe or quotation mark. If you don't specify a name when you create a new field, Works assigns a nondescriptive name like "Field 17."

Hiding a Field Name in Form View

In **form view**, the field name (followed by a colon) appears to the left of each field. If you don't want to see the name (you might want to replace it with something more descriptive), switch to **form design view,** select the field, and then choose the Format Show Field Name command.

Fields

A field is a single piece of information in a **database**, such as Last Name, City, or Price. When you display a database in **list view**, each column is a field; the **field name** is at the top of the document window. In **form view**, each field appears next to its field name.

Adding Fields; Deleting Fields

Filenames

You give a document a name when you choose the File Save or File Save As command. Thanks to Windows 95's long filename capability, only a few file-naming rules apply:

- A filename can't be longer than 250 characters, plus a three-character extension.

- Filenames can contain letters, numbers, spaces, and most symbols, but not the handful of symbols that Windows reserves for other purposes:

" * / : < > ? \ ¦

Works automatically assigns an appropriate extension for the document. If you export a document for use in another program, Works uses that program's extension; if you save a document in the Works format, Works uses one of the following extensions:

Module	Extension
Word processor	WPS
Spreadsheet	WKS
Database	WDB
Communications	WCM

Exporting Documents; Saving Documents

F

Filling Cells You can copy the contents of one or more **cells** into adjacent cells by choosing the Edit Fill Down or Edit Fill Right command. Follow these steps:

1 Highlight the cells you want to copy and the cells where you want the copies to end up.

2 Choose the Edit Fill Down command to copy the contents of the first row of highlighted cells into each of the highlighted cells below, or choose Edit Fill Right to copy the contents of the first column of highlighted cells into each of the highlighted cells to the right.

Updating references

When a cell you copy contains a **relative cell reference**, the reference is adjusted in each of the copies. For example, if cell B10 contains the formula =SUM(B2:B9) and you use Edit Fill Right, cell C10 will contain =SUM(C2:C9).

 Copying Data; Copying Formulas; Fill Series; Selecting Cells

Fill Series You can fill a range of **cells** with a series of numbers or dates. Use this feature if you want to create a list of even numbers, for example, or list a series of dates, such as every other Friday. Here's how:

1 Enter the series' first value in the cell where you want the series to begin.

2 Select the range of cells where you want the series.

3 Choose the Edit Fill Series command.

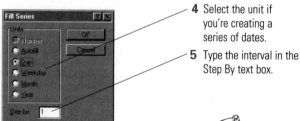

4 Select the unit if you're creating a series of dates.

5 Type the interval in the Step By text box.

F

Filtering Records

A filter searches your **database** to find **records** that meet criteria you specify. You might, for example, want to list all your customers who live in California and who don't smoke. When you apply a filter, Works hides the records that don't match your filter criteria, leaving the records that do match visible in **list view** and **form view**. (And when you create **reports** or use **mail merge** to print **envelopes** or **mailing labels**, Works includes only the visible records, so a filter is a good way to select the records to include in those operations.)

Creating a Filter

1 Choose the Tools Filters command.

2 If you have already created one or more filters in this database, click the New Filter button.

3 Type a name for your new filter (15 characters or less) and click OK.

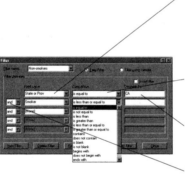

4 In the Field Name drop-down list box, click the down arrow and select the **field** you want to use for the first criterion.

5 Select an option from the Comparison drop-down list.

6 In the Compare To text box, type the text that you want to compare.

7 If you want to add another criterion, select And or Or at the beginning of the next line. If you select And, a record satisfies the filter only if *both* criteria are true. If you select Or, a record satisfies the filter if *either* criterion is true.

8 Repeat steps 4 through 7 to define up to five criteria if you want.

9 Click Apply Filter, and Works hides the records that do not match your filter.

continues

Filtering Records *(continued)*

Wildcards

You can use wildcards in the Compare To box to widen the scope of your filter. Works recognizes two wildcards: a question mark (?) represents any single character, and an asterisk (*) represents any number of characters. To find either "Beatles" or "Beetles," for example, type *Be?tles*.

Reusing a Filter

Works saves up to eight filters with a database document. To reuse a filter you've previously created, choose the Record Apply Filter command and select the filter name from the submenu.

Deleting a Filter

If you want to create a new filter when the database already has eight filters, you must delete one. To do so, choose the Tools Filters command, select the name of the filter, and click Delete Filter. Click Close when you're finished deleting filters.

⁘ **Finding Records; Hiding Records**

Financial Functions

Works has 11 financial **functions** that can quickly calculate depreciation, investment returns, and so on. Do you want to know what your monthly payment will be on the new Land Rover? Enter this formula, which calculates the payment for a $30,000 loan at 9% annual interest, to be paid off in 60 easy monthly payments:

=PMT(30000, 9%/12, 60)

This should pique your interest

Avoid a common error: Be sure that the interest rate argument is for the period specified in the period argument. For example, if the period is monthly, use the monthly interest rate—not the annual interest rate. (That's why I divided the 9% annual rate by 12 in the preceding example.)

 Arguments

Finding Cells

Choose the Edit Find command to locate the next cell that contains the information you specify.

Works begins its search in the upper left corner of the selection. Use the Search radio buttons to specify whether Works should search across the spreadsheet first (mark By Rows) or down the spreadsheet (By Columns).

Use the Look In radio buttons to tell Works whether to look in each cell's **formula**, or in the **value** produced by the formula.

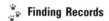 **Finding Records**

Finding Files

Can't find a file? Need to delete some files because your disk is full? Works can launch the Windows 95 Find application, which helps you find files and lets you view, open, rename, move, copy, or delete them. To use it, follow these steps:

1 In the **Works Task Launcher**, click the Existing Documents tab.

2 Click Help Me Find A Document. This opens the Find window, a feature of Windows 95.

3 If you know the name of the file—or part of it—type it in the Named text box.

3 4 5 6   7

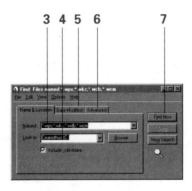

4 If you know which drive contains the file, select it in the Look In box. Otherwise, select My Computer.

5 If you know when you last saved the document, click the Date Modified tab and specify the date.

6 If you're looking for a file that contains specific text, click the Advanced tab and enter the text in the Containing Text box.

7 Click Find Now.

Find displays its results at the bottom of the Find window. Double-click the name of the document you're looking for to open it in Works, or **right-click** it and select another option (such as Quick View, Delete, or Rename) from the **shortcut menu**.

F

Finding Records

To quickly and simply find a **record** that contains certain text, choose the Edit Find command. Type the text you're looking for—Works ignores capitalization in its search—and Works selects the next **field** that contains the text.

A simple filter

You can also use the Edit Find command to view all the records that contain the text you're looking for. In the Find dialog box, mark All Records. Works then displays only the records that contain the text you specify, and hides the rest.

Filtering Records; Hiding Records

Finding Text

Choose the Edit Find command to locate phrases, words, or other snippets of text in a word processor document. Before you use the Edit Find command, select the document area that you want Works to search; if you want to search the entire document, be sure that no text is selected.

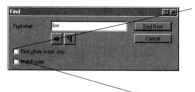

Mark the Find Whole Words Only check box if you want Works to ignore occurrences of the Find What text that are contained within a longer word.

Mark the Match Case check box if you want Works to find only text that matches exactly—including capitalization.

continues

73

Finding Text *(continued)*

Finding Special Characters

Besides locating letters, numbers, and punctuation, the Edit Find command can search for **nonprinting characters** and other funny symbols.

Click the ➡ button to add a tab character to the search string, or click ¶ to add a paragraph mark. Or type any of the these codes:

To search for	Type this in the Find What box
An end-of-line mark	^n
A **paragraph** mark	^p
A **page break**	^d
A tab character	^t
A **nonbreaking space**	^s
White space (tab characters or spaces)	^w
Any character	?
A question mark	^?
A caret (^)	^^

∴ **Finding Cells; Finding Records; Selecting Text**

Fonts

 You can use a variety of fonts (type styles) in your Works documents. In addition to the fonts included with Windows, Works includes many others. And a visit to any software store or shareware forum will present thousands more.

To view a sample of the fonts installed on your system, click the down arrow by the Font Name drop-down list and scroll through the list. (Some symbol fonts might be unreadable, but if you select one its name will be legible at the top of the list.)

∴ **Changing Fonts**

Footnotes
Footnotes, which appear at the bottom of the page, are used for documenting quotations or for making incidental comments that you don't want to include in the main text.

Adding a Footnote

1 Place the **insertion point** where you want the footnote reference to appear.

2 Choose the Insert Footnote command. Works displays the Insert Footnote dialog box.

3 Select the Numbered radio button if you want Works to number footnotes consecutively, or select Special Mark and enter the character if you want to use a symbol such as an asterisk as the footnote marker.

4 Click Insert. Works displays the footnote at the bottom of the window and places the insertion point there so you can type your footnote text.

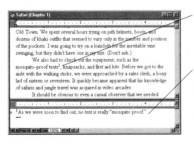

Footnote reference

In normal view, footnotes appear in a separate footnote pane. To open it, choose View Footnotes.

Deleting a Footnote

To delete a footnote, select the footnote marker and press Del. The footnote is deleted from the footnote area, and the remaining footnotes are automatically renumbered.

❖ **Endnotes; Window Panes**

Formatting

The Bible admonishes, "Judge not according to the appearance" (John 7:24), but judicious formatting sure makes documents easier to read.

Adding borders and shading ⁘ **Borders; Shading**

Changing colors ⁘ **Borders; Changing Fonts; Chart Formatting; Shading**

Changing font styles ⁘ **Bold Characters; Changing Fonts; Fonts; Italic Characters; Underline Characters**

Formatting charts ⁘ **Chart Formatting; Charts; Chart Text; Chart Types**

Formatting database forms ⁘ **Alignment; Formatting Fields; Field Lines; Field Names**

Formatting numbers and dates ⁘ **Alignment; Currency Symbols; Date Formats; Formatting Fields; Formatting Numbers; Fractions; Percentages; Scientific Notation; Time Formats**

Formatting pages ⁘ **Headers and Footers; Margins; Page Numbers; Page Orientation; Page Setup**

Formatting paragraphs ⁘ **Bulleted Lists; Indents and Alignment; Line Spacing; Paragraph Breaks**

Formatting reports ⁘ **Alignment; Borders; Changing Fonts; Column Width; Formatting Numbers; Headers and Footers; Margins; Page Numbers; Page Orientation; Page Setup; Row Height**

Formatting spreadsheets and tables ⁘ **Alignment; AutoFormat; Column Width; Gridlines; Row Height**

Setting tab stops ⁘ **Tabs**

F

Formatting Fields In **list view** or **form design view**, you can choose the Format Field command to change the **field name**, select a format, or set a default value.

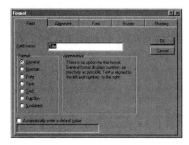

✦ Adding Fields; Entering Data; Formatting Numbers

Formatting Numbers 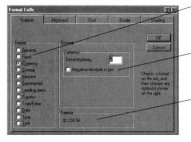 You can format numbers and dates by selecting the **cells** you want to format and choosing the Format Number command.

Use the Format radio buttons to select a formatting category.

Works displays the options available for the selected format.

Works displays a sample that shows how your current selections in the Format and Options boxes might look.

Formatting when you enter data

Sometimes it's easier to format numbers and dates by entering the **value** in the format you want. For example, if you enter *$1,000.00* into a cell, the cell contains the value 1000, but Works automatically formats it to include a dollar sign, comma, and two decimal places.

F

Form Design View

Form design view lets you create and modify **forms**, which you use in **form view**. To switch to form design view, press Ctrl+F9, click the Form Design tool, or choose the View Form Design command.

Creating a Form

Works has several **TaskWizards** that can lead you through the process of creating a form, or you can follow these steps:

1 In the **Works Task Launcher**, click the Works Tools tab and click Database.

2 In the Create Database dialog box, create your **fields** by entering a **field name**, selecting a format (and any options), and clicking Add. Click Done when you're finished adding fields.

3 Press Ctrl+F9 to switch to form design view.

4 Modify the form as you want.

- To insert a new field, position the **insertion point** where you want the field. Type the field name followed by a colon and then press Enter. Works displays the Insert Field dialog box, where you can select a format, appearance options, and a default value.

- To change a field's position or size, drag the field or its sizing handles.

- To insert text other than a field name, simply position the insertion point and type.

- You can dress up your form by **adding pictures**, **changing fonts**, using **borders**, **shading**, and so on.

- To hide a field name, select it and choose the Format Show Field Name command.

In form design view, Works displays a dotted outline around each field and other objects.

Forms

A form is a screen representation of a paper data-entry form. (But when you add pictures, borders, and fancy fonts, it's more attractive than an ordinary paper form.) When you examine a **database** in **form view**, Works displays one **record** at a time.

Printing blank forms

Your Works form might look so good that you'll want printed copies to use for collecting data. Here's how: In form view, press Ctrl+End to display the blank form after the last record. Then choose the File Print command and select the Current Record Only radio button.

*:• **Entering Data; Form Design View**

Formulas

In Works, you use a formula in a spreadsheet cell or database **field** when you want to calculate a **value**. (You must use **list view** to enter a formula in a database field.) A formula must begin with an equal sign (=), and it can contain values, **cell addresses**, cell **names**, **functions**, and the following arithmetic operators:

Operator	What it does	Example, result
^	Raises to a power	=5^2, 25
*	Multiplies	=5*2, 10
/	Divides	=5/2, 2.5
+	Adds	=5+2, 7
–	Subtracts	=5–2, 3
=	Returns TRUE if equal	=5=2, FALSE
<>	Returns TRUE if not equal	=5<>2, TRUE
<	Returns TRUE if less than	=5<2, FALSE
>	Returns TRUE if greater than	=5>2, TRUE
<=	Returns TRUE if less than or equal to	=5<=2, FALSE
>=	Returns TRUE if greater than or equal to	=5>=2, TRUE

continues

Formulas *(continued)*

The power of formulas, of course, is not determining that 5 is, in fact, greater than 2. More likely, you'll want to perform calculations based on the values in other cells. For example, the formula =C2–C18 subtracts the value in C18 from the value in cell C2.

The easiest way to enter cell addresses is to point to the cell (or cell range) as you enter the formula. After you type = to begin formula entry, selecting cells doesn't change the **active cell**; instead it enters the cell address in the **entry bar**.

Better looking formulas

You can make your formulas easier to read by naming cells before you enter the formula. The previous example could then read =Price–Cost.

:: **Easy Calc**

Form View   Form view is one of the two basic ways to view information in a **database**. (The other is **list view**.) Form view shows a single **record**. Press F9 to switch to form view.

Business Contacts

Business Contacts

Date Entered: _____ (the date you entered data in this form)
Mr./Mrs./Ms.: _____
First Name: David   Last Name: Lanterman
Job Title: Product Manager
Business Name: The Phone Company
Address Line 1: 2005 Broadway Avenue, Suite 703
Address Line 2: _____
City: Santa Monica   State: CA
Postal Code: 90411-8003   Country: _____
Phone 1: (310) 555-0614   Phone 2: _____

To view the next record, click here or press Ctrl+PgDn.

To skip to the blank record at the end, click here or press Ctrl+End.

:: **Field Lines; Views**

Fractions

Normally, Works displays numbers as decimal values. But if you're tracking stock prices or maintaining an inventory that includes shoe sizes, you'll want to see fractions. To display numbers as fractions, select the cells you want and choose the Format Number command. Mark Fraction and, optionally, specify the denominator.

Entering a Fraction

To enter a fractional value, type a space between the integer and the fraction, like this: *4 1/2*.

Entering values less than 1

When you enter a fractional value that is less than 1, be sure to type 0 (zero) and a space before the fraction (for example, *0 3/8*). Otherwise, Works interprets your entry as a date.

> **Formatting Numbers; Selecting Cells**

Functions

A function is a predefined **formula** that makes it much easier to perform complex calculations in a **spreadsheet** or **database**. To use a function, enter its name in a formula. After the name, type the input for the formula enclosed in parentheses. (Each input value is called an "**argument**," but let's not bicker.) If a function requires more than one argument, separate them with a comma. For example:

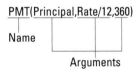

PMT(Principal,Rate/12,360)

Name

Arguments

continues

Functions *(continued)*

Calculations for investments, loans, and depreciation	**Financial Functions**
Conditional tests	**Logical Functions**
Functions for displaying and calculating dates and times	**Date and Time Functions**
Functions for displaying error values	**Informational Functions**
Functions for formatting, finding, and manipulating text strings	**Text Functions**
References to other cells	**Lookup and Reference Functions**
The stuff you never understood in high school	**Mathematical and Trigonometric Functions**
The stuff you never understood in college	**Statistical Functions**

If you always lose arguments

The name and syntax of some Works functions are not easy to remember, but Works can prompt you. In the spreadsheet module, choose the Insert Function command. The Insert Function dialog box lists all the available functions (you can shorten the list by marking a category) and shows the names of the arguments each function requires. Select a function and choose OK to insert it in the **entry bar**.

Easy Calc

Go To 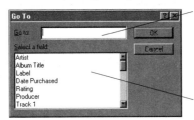 You can jump directly to a specific place in the active document by choosing the Edit Go To command or by using its keyboard shortcut, Ctrl+G:

You can jump directly to a page (word processor), **cell** (spreadsheet), or **record** (database) by typing its number in the Go To text box.

The list box lists all the **bookmarks** (word processor), range **names** (spreadsheet), or **field names** (database) that you have defined; select one to go to it.

Gridlines Gridlines are the dotted lines that delineate the cells in the spreadsheet or in the database **list view**. You can make them appear and disappear by choosing the View Gridlines command.

Printing gridlines

The View Gridlines command controls only the display of gridlines. To control whether gridlines print, choose the File Page Setup command, select the Other Options tab, and use the Print Gridlines check box.

 **Chart Formatting**

Headers and Footers

A header is text that appears at the top of every page; a footer appears at the bottom of every page. You can use headers and footers to print page numbers, titles, filenames, dates, and other information.

Creating Headers and Footers in Spreadsheet and Database Documents

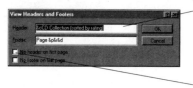

1 Choose the View Headers And Footers command.

2 Type the text you want for the header and footer. You can include any of the codes shown below.

3 Mark these check boxes if you want the header or footer to print on all pages except the first page.

To do this	Insert this code
Left align characters that follow	&l
Right align characters that follow	&r
Center characters that follow	&c
Print the page number	&p
Print the filename	&f
Print the date	&d
Print the date in long format	&n
Print the time	&t
Print a single ampersand	&&

Creating Headers or Footers in Word Processor Documents

In the word processor, headers and footers can contain multiple lines and pictures, and you can use all the word processor's formatting capabilities. To create such a header while in page layout **view,** simply scroll to the top of the page (to create a header) or the bottom of the page (to create a footer). Then click in the box labeled "Header" or "Footer," and begin typing.

If you prefer normal view, scroll to the top of the document, where you'll find the header and footer paragraphs identified with an *H* or *F* in the left margin.

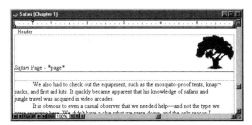

But first ...

If you want the header or footer to print on all pages except the first page, choose the File Page Setup command and click the Other Options tab. Then select the No Header (or Footer) On First Page check box.

Margins; Page Numbers

Help   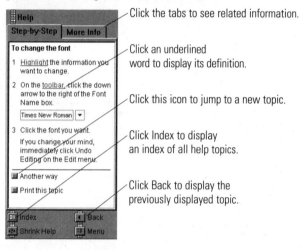 Works displays help about the module or dialog box you're currently using in a panel at the right side of the Works window. Check here first when you have a question. Within that panel, you'll find several places to click to get more information.

Click the tabs to see related information.

Click an underlined word to display its definition.

Click this icon to jump to a new topic.

Click Index to display an index of all help topics.

Click Back to display the previously displayed topic.

Help me get help out of the way

You can reduce the help panel to a narrow column by clicking the Shrink Help button at the bottom of the help panel. (What? You thought that offered assistance from a psychiatrist?) Restore the full panel by clicking Shrink Help again.

If you want to get rid of the help panel altogether, choose the Help Hide Help command; choose Help Show Help to reopen it. And if you find that you no longer need to have help always visible, choose the Tools Options command and click the View tab. Clear the Show Help At Startup check box and you won't need to use Help Hide Help each time you start Works.

H

Hiding Fields

 In **list view**, you'll sometimes find it useful to hide one or more **fields** so you can view nonadjacent fields side by side. To do so, drag the **field name's** right border to the left until you can no longer see the field. Alternatively, you can select the field and then choose the Format Field Width command. Set the width to 0.

Restoring Hidden Fields

If you want to display a field in list view that you have hidden, follow these steps:

1 Choose the Edit Go To command.

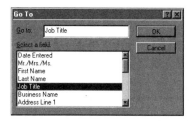

2 Select the name of the field you want to restore, and then click OK.

3 Choose the Format Field Width command.

4 Click Standard, click Best Fit, or enter a width greater than 0 and click OK.

Hiding Records

You can hide **records** that you're not interested in viewing. Hidden records do not print, nor are they included in **reports**, form letters, **mailing labels**, or other **mail merge** operations.

Hiding Records

You can hide certain records in any of these ways:

- Choose the Edit Find command and mark All Records. Works hides the records that don't contain the search text you specify.

- Use a query. Works hides records that don't satisfy the query.

- Select one or more records and choose the Record Hide Record command. (In **form view**, you can hide only one record at a time with this method.)

Viewing Hidden Records

You can make all the hidden records visible and make all the visible records hidden by choosing the Record Show Hidden Records command.

To make all records visible again, choose the Record Show All Records command.

Filtering Records; Finding Records

Hyphenation

Works can automatically hyphenate words in your document, which reduces the raggedness of the right margin. To do so, choose the Tools Hyphenation command.

Mark the Hyphenate CAPS check box if it's OK to hyphenate words that are all uppercase.

Mark the Confirm check box if you want Works to stop and show you each proposed hyphen, giving you an opportunity to change its position or prevent hyphenation of a word.

The Hot Zone balances the number of hyphens vs. raggedness. A narrow hot zone hyphenates more words to make the margin less ragged; a wide hot zone results in fewer hyphens and a more ragged margin.

Optional hyphens and nonbreaking hyphens

An optional hyphen is one that the **word wrap** feature in Works uses only if it falls near the end of the line; otherwise it is invisible. The Tools Hyphenation command inserts optional hyphens where it deems necessary. You can also insert an optional hyphen by pressing Ctrl+hyphen.

Sometimes you'll want to be sure that a certain hyphen doesn't fall at the end of a line, such as the hyphen in a compound name. In this case, use a nonbreaking hyphen. Press Ctrl+Shift+hyphen.

Importing Files

Exporting Documents; Opening Documents

Indents and Alignment  Indents are the space between the text and the page margins; alignment refers to the way text lines up with the margins. You control paragraph indents and alignment with the Format Paragraph command.

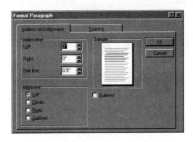

Use predefined indents and alignment

Choose the Format Easy Formats command to see a list of predefined paragraph formats—saving you the effort of specifying indents, alignment, and **line spacing**.

Informational Functions  The four informational **functions** work with cells that contain the **value** ERR (for "error") or N/A ("not available"). For example, the following **formula** displays 1 (TRUE) if cell A5 contains N/A; otherwise it displays 0 (FALSE):

=ISNA(A5)

Naaah

To obtain the value N/A, you must use the NA() function. If you simply type *N/A* in the **entry bar**, Microsoft Works interprets it as text instead of a special value.

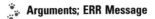 **Arguments; ERR Message**

Inserting Columns and Rows To insert a new column or row in a spreadsheet, **right-click** a **cell** or **range.** From the **shortcut menu,** choose the Insert Column command to insert a new column to the left of the highlighted cell, or choose Insert Row to insert a row above the highlighted cell.

Inserting multiple columns or rows

To insert more than one column or row, select multiple cells before choosing the Insert Row or Insert Column command. Works inserts one column or row for each selected column or row.

∴ **Adding Fields; Adding Records**

Inserting Fields

∴ **Adding Fields; Mail Merge**

Insertion Point The insertion point is the flashing vertical bar that shows where the characters you type will appear. You can move the insertion point by using the direction keys, or by clicking where you want the insertion point to be.

Italic Characters To change characters to *italic*, select the text (or the cells that contain the text) and then press Ctrl+I or click the Italic tool.

L

Labels

 Chart Text; Mailing Labels

Letterheads To create and use a custom letterhead, follow these steps:

1 In the **Works Task Launcher**, click the TaskWizards tab.

2 Select Letterhead (in the Common Tasks category) and click OK. The **TaskWizard** guides you through the process of creating a letterhead.

3 Make any modifications you want to the letterhead document.

4 Choose the File Save As command and then click the Template button.

5 Type a name for your **template** and click OK.

Thereafter, to create a letter, open the Works Task Launcher and select your letterhead template (in the User Defined Templates category). Click OK to create a new document using your custom letterhead.

Line Spacing To adjust the space between the lines in a **paragraph**, before the paragraph, or after the paragraph, select the paragraph and then choose the Format Paragraph command. Click the Spacing tab.

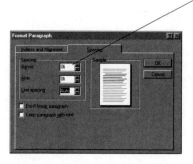

Enter a number in each of the three Spacing text boxes. If you enter a number alone, Works interprets it as a number of lines. (There are six lines per inch.) You can also specify spacing in inches (in or "), centimeters (cm), picas (pi), **points** (pt), or millimeters (mm) by appending the unit abbreviation to the number.

Using Auto spacing

If you type "Auto" in the Line Spacing text box, Works sets the line spacing to the height of the tallest character in each line.

Row Height

Lists

Bulleted Lists

List View

 List view is one of the two basic ways to view information in a **database**. (The other is **form view**.) List view displays the information in a **spreadsheet**-like format, where each **record** occupies one **row** and each **column** represents a **field**.

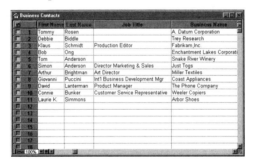

Gridlines; Views

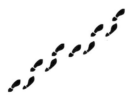

Logical Functions Works has six logical **functions**, which are based on the theory that everything—at least in the world of spreadsheets—is either true or false. In fact—except for the IF() function—the logical functions can return only one of two answers: 1 (TRUE) or 0 (FALSE). Logical functions are typically used to check for the presence (or absence) of certain conditions. The following example **formula** displays one message if the value of the range named Profit is greater than $10,000, and a different message if it is not:

=IF(Profit>10000,"Great news!","Uh-oh")

Displaying logical values as text

Normally, Works displays the result of a logical function as either 0 or 1. You can make your spreadsheet more legible by **formatting numbers** as True/False. Then cells that contain the value 0 display as FALSE; cells that contain any other numeric value display as TRUE.

∴ Arguments

Lookup and Reference Functions The six lookup and reference **functions** can do things like tell you how many columns are in a range you specify or look up a **value** from a list or from a **range** of **cells**. For example, this **formula** displays "Better" if the value of cell B5 is 2:

=CHOOSE(B5,"Good","Better","Best")

∴ Arguments

Lotus 1-2-3 Lotus 1-2-3 is another **spreadsheet** program.
Why mention it here? Because you can open and save Lotus 1-2-3 version 2.*x* worksheet files with Works. To do so, choose the File Open or File Save As command, and then select Lotus 1-2-3 in the Files Of Type list box.

❖❖ **Exporting Documents; Opening Documents; Saving Documents**

Mailing Labels You can create labels from within a word processor or database document by choosing the Tools Labels command. (If you choose this command from the database module, Works automatically opens a word processor document, which is where you'll actually create the labels.) But a faster way is to choose a **TaskWizard** from the **Works Task Launcher.**

Printing One or More Copies of a Single Label

1 In the Works Task Launcher, click the TaskWizards tab.

2 Select Return Address Labels (in the Envelopes and Labels category) and click OK.

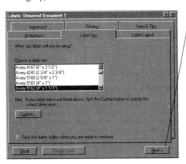

3 Follow the TaskWizard's lead by filling out each tab in the dialog box and then clicking Next >.

4 When you've completed the steps, click Close. You can then edit, format, and embellish your label using the usual word processor tools before you print.

5 To print your labels, choose the File Print command and select the Mailing Labels radio button. Then click OK.

continues

Mailing Labels *(continued)*

Printing Labels from a Database

1 In the Works Task Launcher, click the TaskWizards tab.

2 Select Labels (in the Envelopes and Labels category) and click OK.

3 As the TaskWizard presents each tab in the dialog box, select a label size, select a database, and select which records to print. Click Next after you complete each tab.

4 In the Label Layout tab, for each field you want to print on the label, click its name and then click Add Field to insert a placeholder in the Label Layout text box.

5 Click New Line to insert a line break.

6 Insert punctuation and other text as needed to separate the placeholders in the Label Layout text box.

7 Click Next to reach the Printing tab and specify the number of copies of each label. If you're starting with a partial sheet of labels, you can also specify the row to start in.

8 Click Print to print the labels immediately, or click Close to create a document, which you can format and edit before printing.

Selecting Avery labels

The Label Size tab shows lots of Avery labels. The 4000-series labels are for dot-matrix printers, and the 5000-series labels are for laser and inkjet printers. The other Avery products shown are metric sizes that are generally available only outside the United States.

Mail Merge With the merge capabilities in Works, you can print a word processor document, such as a form letter or **envelope,** for every **record** in a **database**. As usual, the easiest way to get started is with a **TaskWizard**. From the **Works Task Launcher,** select Letter (in the Common Tasks category).

After you create a letter or other document, you can add database fields anywhere in the document. Follow these steps:

1   To include the contents of a **field** from the database, choose the Insert Database Field command. (The first time you choose Insert Database Field, the Current Database box might show None. Click the Use A Different Database button and then select a database from the list that appears.)

2   Select the field you want and click Insert. Works inserts a placeholder in the document. Insert all the field placeholders you want; you can move and format them later. Choose Close when you're finished inserting field placeholders.

continues

Mail Merge *(continued)*

3 Format your document—including the field placeholders.

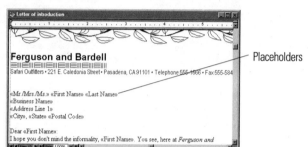

Placeholders

4 If you don't want to print a document for every record in a database, open the database and hide the records you don't want to include. You can hide records manually or with a filter.

5 To print your documents (that's right, *documents*—one for each nonhidden record), switch to the word processor document and choose File Print. Be sure the Print Merge check box is marked before you choose OK.

∴ **Filtering Records; Hiding Records; Mailing Labels**

Manual Calculation Works normally recalculates all the **values** that change whenever you make an entry in a **cell**, which can slow you down if you have a very large spreadsheet. To tell Works to wait, choose the Tools Options command. Click the Data Entry tab, and then select the Use Manual Calculation check box. Then, when you want Works to calculate the spreadsheet, press F9.

M

Margins

Margins control the white space around the edge of a page. To set the margins, choose the File Page Setup command and select the Margins tab.

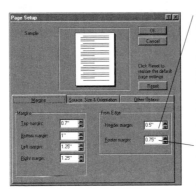

The Header Margin sets the distance between the top of the page and the top of the header. This entry must be smaller than the Top Margin, which specifies the distance from the top of the page to the top of the text.

The Footer Margin sets the distance from the bottom of the page to the top of the footer. This entry must be smaller than the Bottom Margin —the distance from the bottom of the page to the bottom of the text.

Headers and Footers; Indents and Alignment

Marking Records

Sometimes you'll want to select **records** that don't neatly fit a filter criteria (for example, "records for the labels that came off inside the printer"). Switch to **list view,** and then click the check box at the left end of each record you want to mark. Choose Record Show Marked Records to hide the unmarked records, and you're ready to reprint those labels—after you extract the first batch from the printer!

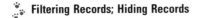

Click here to mark (or unmark) all records.

Click here to mark (or unmark) an individual record.

Filtering Records; Hiding Records

Mathematical and Trigonometric Functions

Works has 17 **functions** that calculate logarithms, sines, square roots, and other fun things that can make complex mathematical **formulas**. Here's a sampling of what they can do:

Function	What it does
=INT(3.8)	Returns the integer portion of 3.8, which is 3
=LOG(100)	Returns the common logarithm of 100, which is 2
=SIN(1)	Returns the sine of 1, which is 0.841471
=PI()	Returns the value of π, which is 3.1415927

 Arguments

Microsoft Excel

Microsoft Excel is a **spreadsheet** program—the "big brother" of the spreadsheet and charting module in Works. It does everything Works does and then some. And then some more. But it's not my job to sell Excel; I mention it here because you might find it handy to use Works on your home or portable computer and Excel on your desktop computer. You'll see lots of similarities, and you can open and save your Excel worksheets in Works. You can also open Works spreadsheets in Excel.

Keep it simple

Did I mention that Excel has many more features and capabilities than Works? When you use Excel with a worksheet that you'll later open in Works, be sure you use only the features and **functions** supported by Works. If you insert one of Excel's convoluted functions, for example, Works changes it to its last calculated value when you open the spreadsheet in Works.

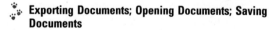

 Exporting Documents; Opening Documents; Saving Documents

Microsoft Word

Microsoft Word is a word processor that does things you never imagined a word processor could do. And it coexists nicely with Works: Many of the menus, toolbar buttons, dialog boxes, and procedures are nearly the same, so it's easy to move back and forth between the programs. And your word processor documents can move back and forth easily too; you can open and save Word for Windows documents in Works.

Exporting Documents; Opening Documents; Saving Documents

Mixed Cell References

A mixed reference combines an **absolute cell reference** and a **relative cell reference**, allowing you to refer to cells so that only the **column** or only the **row** reference is absolute. Place a dollar sign ($) before the part of the reference that you want to be absolute. For example, B$6 contains a relative column reference (B) and an absolute row reference ($6).

If you copy a **cell** that contains such a reference, the absolute row or column reference remains unchanged, and the relative reference adjusts.

Moving Data

You can move data within a **database** or spreadsheet the same way you move text in a word processor document: You use **drag and drop**, or use Edit Cut and Edit Paste.

Copying Data

Moving Objects and Pictures

You can move objects (such as **Note-It** notes, **tables**, and **charts**) and pictures within a document by selecting the object and dragging it where you want it. Alternatively, you can use the Edit Cut and Edit Paste commands.

Copying Objects and Pictures; Drag and Drop; Selecting Objects

Moving Text  The easiest way to move selected text is to drag it to the desired location.

You can also move text by following these steps:

1 Select the text you want to move.

2 Choose the Edit Cut command, which removes the text from the document and places it on the **Clipboard**.

3 Place the **insertion point** where you want the text.

4 Choose the Edit Paste command.

Drag and Drop; Copying Text; Selecting Text

Names  You can name a **cell** or a **range** of cells and then use that name in **formulas** and dialog boxes instead of using a **cell address**. To name a cell or a range, follow these steps:

1 Select the cell or range of cells.

2 Choose the Insert Range Name command. Works displays the Range Name dialog box.

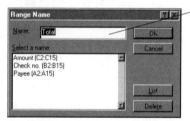

3 Type the name in the Name text box. Range names can be up to 15 characters long. Existing range names appear in the Names list box.

4 Click OK.

Use labels as range names

If the topmost or leftmost cell in the highlighted range contains a label (in other words, text), Works proposes that text as the range name when you choose the Insert Range Name command.

Field Names; Filenames

New Documents

To create a new document, choose the—what else?—File New command to display the **Works Task Launcher**.

    Opening Documents

Nonbreaking Spaces

A nonbreaking space ensures that two words stay together on the same line. To insert a nonbreaking space, press Ctrl+Shift+Spacebar or choose the Insert Special Character command.

    Special Characters

Nonprinting Characters

Some **special characters** determine the appearance of a document by controlling, for example, where lines end and how words are hyphenated. Normally, these nonprinting characters do not appear on the screen, but you can see them by choosing the View All Characters command.

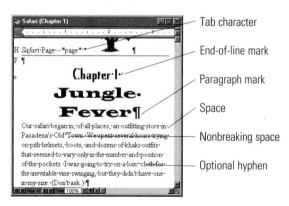

- Tab character
- End-of-line mark
- Paragraph mark
- Space
- Nonbreaking space
- Optional hyphen

    Ending Lines; Hyphenation; Nonbreaking Spaces; Paragraphs

Note-It

Note-It is an accessory application that lets you put pop-up notes—identified by a cute icon of your choosing—in your word processor documents and database **forms**.

Creating a Note-It Note

Place the **insertion point** in the word processor document or database form where you want the note picture to appear, and then choose the Insert Note-It command.

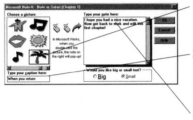

1 Select the picture that you want to mark your note.

2 Type the caption that you want to appear beneath the note picture.

3 Type the text that you want to pop up when you open the note.

Reading a Note-It Note

Simply double-click the note picture, and your note text pops up in a separate window. To close the note window, click anywhere or press any key.

— This note pops up

— When you double-click here

Deleting Objects; Moving Objects and Pictures; OLE Linking and Embedding; Resizing Objects and Pictures

O

OLE Linking and Embedding 📄🖥 OLE linking and
embedding, commonly abbreviated as OLE (as in ¡Olé!),
is a feature of Microsoft Windows. OLE lets you create a
"compound document"—one that combines two or
more types of information. You use this feature (perhaps
unknowingly) to place a **table, Note-It** note, or **ClipArt
Gallery** picture in a word processor document, for example.

Creating a Compound Document

You'll never see "OLE" or "OLE linking and embedding" on a Works
menu. Instead, you use the Insert menu, which has commands for most
of the commonly used objects. The Insert Object command is a catchall
that lets you insert any type of object that's available on your system.
(*Object* is the technical term for the thing-from-another-application-
that-you-want-to-place-in-a-document.)

Working with Objects

If you click an object in a Works document, a rectangular frame
surrounds the object, and you can then copy, move, delete, or resize
the object. If you double-click the object, the application that created
the object takes over. With most object types, that means the
application's menus and toolbar appear, and you can edit the object—
all from within Works. When you're finished editing, just click outside
the object, and the standard Works menu returns.

Creating objects ❖ **Drag and Drop; Embedding and Linking
Existing Objects; Embedding New Objects; Sharing Works
Data**

Modifying objects ❖ **Deleting Objects; Moving Objects and
Pictures; Resizing Objects and Pictures**

0

Opening Documents 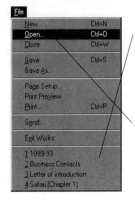 To open a previously saved Works document, follow these steps:

1 Open the File menu. If the document you want to open is among the last four you used, its name appears at the bottom of the File menu and you can reopen it simply by choosing its name from this menu.

2 If the document isn't listed, choose the Open command.

3 Use the Files Of Type list box if you want to open a file that was saved in a format other than the Works format.

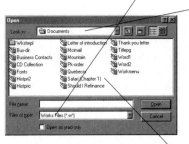

4 If the file you want isn't listed, double-click a folder icon to open a subfolder of the current folder, or press F4 to open the Look In drop-down list, which allows you to view the contents of a different drive or folder.

5 Select the filename or type it in the File Name text box and click Open.

O

Protecting your original document

Sometimes you'll want to be sure that you don't inadvertently change a previously saved document. You can protect a document by marking the Open As Read-Only check box in the Open dialog box. Works won't prevent you from making changes to the document while it's open, but you won't be able to resave it using the same name. You'll either have to abandon your changes or save the file under a new name—keeping the original file intact.

 New Documents; Works Task Launcher

Options The Options dialog box lets you make default settings for a handful of unrelated options—most of which you'll never need to change. To see what you can change, choose the Tools Options command.

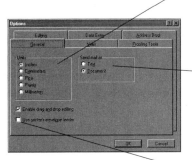

The Units section determines the units of measure that appear on the **ruler**, in **formatting** and **Page Setup** dialog boxes, and so on.

If you use electronic mail to send Works documents to other users, mark Document if the recipient also has Works; otherwise mark Text.

If your printer has an envelope feeder, mark this box before you print **envelopes**.

Page Borders

Jazz up certificates and other documents by adding a border around the page. Just follow these steps:

1 Choose the Format Borders And Shading command.
2 Click the Page tab.

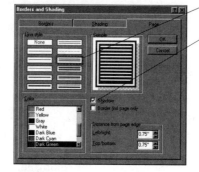

3 Select a line style and color for the border.

4 Mark the Shadow check box if you want to add a shadow to the lower right corner, which gives the border a three-dimensional appearance.

5 Click OK.

Crossing the border

If the page border overlaps your document text or the **headers and footers**, you can adjust the position of the border or the position of the text to fix the problem. To move the border, adjust the Distance From Page Edge settings on the Page tab of the Borders And Shading dialog box. To move the document text, choose the File Page Setup command and adjust the **margins**.

Page Breaks

A page break determines where a new page begins when you print a document. Works figures out the location of page breaks automatically—but you can override its actions.

Page Breaks in Word Processor Documents

In normal view, automatic page breaks are indicated by a » symbol in the left margin.

To insert a manual page break, press Ctrl+Enter. A dotted line across the window indicates a manual page break, which you can delete or move like any other character.

You can restrict automatic page breaks so that certain paragraphs are not separated by a page break. See **Paragraph Breaks**.

Page Breaks in Spreadsheets, Database List View, and Reports

To insert a manual page break in a spreadsheet or a database's **list view** or **report view**, select the **row** (**record**) below or the **column** (**field**) to the right of where you want to insert a page break. Then choose Insert Page Break. Works indicates a manual page break with a dashed line.

To delete a manual page break, select the row below or the column to the right of the page break. Then choose the Insert Delete Page Break command.

Page Breaks in Database Forms

To insert a manual page break in a database **form**, switch to **form design view,** place the **insertion point** where you want the page break, and choose Format Insert Page Break. Works indicates the page break with a dotted line across the window.

Works normally prints each database form on a new page. If you prefer to save a tree and print as many forms as will fit on each sheet, choose the File Page Setup command and select the Other Options tab. Then clear the Page Breaks Between Records check box.

 Finding Text; Special Characters

Page Numbers You can number the pages of any
spreadsheet or database document you print by including
the &p code in the header or footer.

In a word processor document, you can insert a page
number anywhere. To do so, choose the Insert Page
Number command.

Setting the beginning page number

If you want to start numbering pages with a number other than 1,
choose File Page Setup and select the Other Options tab. Then type
the number you want in the Starting Page Number box.

Headers and Footers

Page Orientation You can print your pages in ei-
ther portrait (vertical) or landscape (horizontal) orientation. To select the orientation, choose the File Page Setup
command and select the Source, Size & Orientation tab.

Page Setup Choose the File Page Setup command
to display the Page Setup dialog box, which lets you set
margins, header and footer locations, paper size, **page
orientation,** beginning **page number,** and sundry print-
related options for each Works module.

**Endnotes; Field Lines; Footnotes; Gridlines; Page Breaks;
Reports**

Pagination Microsoft Works automatically figures
out where each printed page in a document should begin.
You can override its choices by putting in your own **page
breaks** or by restricting **paragraph breaks**.

Paragraph Breaks

You can prevent Works from splitting a **paragraph** over a page boundary, and you can ensure that two paragraphs are not separated by a page boundary. To do so, select the paragraphs you want to control, choose Format Paragraph, and select the Spacing tab.

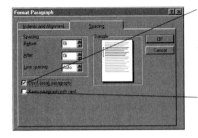

Mark the Don't Break Paragraph check box to prevent Works from placing an automatic **page break** within the selected paragraphs.

Mark the Keep Paragraph With Next check box to prevent Works from placing an automatic page break between the selected paragraphs and the paragraph that follows. (Headings, for example, benefit from this setting, because they look really dumb when they are at the bottom of a page.)

Paragraphs

A paragraph (at least as Works views it) is some text—words, sentences, whatever—that ends with a paragraph mark. You insert a paragraph mark by pressing Enter. (Choose View All Characters to see the paragraph marks, which look like this: ¶.)

It's important to think of paragraphs in the same way that Works does, because **formatting** and **pagination** are based on paragraphs.

Indents and Alignment; Line Spacing; Paragraph Breaks

Paragraph Spacing

> ⁖ **Line Spacing; Resizing Fields; Row Height**

Pasting

You can copy the contents of the Clipboard to the active window by choosing Edit Paste, pressing Ctrl+V, or clicking the Paste tool. The **Clipboard** contents are inserted at the **insertion point** or in the **active cell**. If you have selected text, the Clipboard contents replace the selection.

For additional paste options, choose Edit Paste Special. The dialog box that appears varies, depending on the contents of the Clipboard and the module you are pasting into, but as you select the different options, an explanation in the dialog box spells out what'll happen if you choose OK.

> ⁖ **OLE Linking and Embedding**

Patterns

> ⁖ **Chart Formatting; Shading**

Percentages

Percentages are decimal **values**, such as 0.15, that are formatted like this: 15%. To enter a percentage in a **cell**, you can enter its decimal value and then format it. Or you can simply type it as a percentage, including the percent sign (%).

> ⁖ **Formatting Numbers**

Phone Settings

Before you can connect to another computer, you need to tell Works how to make the connection. You do so by choosing the Settings Phone command.

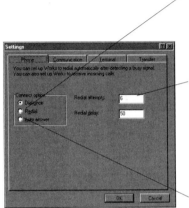

Select the Redial radio button if you want Works to retry if it can't connect the first time—such as when it gets a busy signal.

If you select the Redial radio button, you can also specify the number of times you want Works to retry before giving up altogether—and the amount of time (in seconds) to wait between attempts.

If you want your modem to answer incoming calls, select Auto Answer. Works then ignores the other settings in the Phone Settings dialog box.

Communication Settings; Protocol; Terminal Settings

P

Points

A point is a unit of measure used by printers and typographers to specify the size of type. A point is about 1/72 of an inch. The type size shown on the **toolbar** and in the Format Font And Style dialog box is expressed in points. You can also use points to specify other measurements, such as the size of **margins**. To do so, append the abbreviation pt to the numeric measurement.

: Changing Fonts

Positioning Fields

In **form design view**, you can move a database **field** and its **field name**. Click the field to select it, and then drag it to its new location.

Line up, everybody

Forms look better when the fields are aligned with each other. To facilitate alignment, be sure the Format Snap To Grid command is checked. (Choose it if it isn't checked.) This creates an invisible 12-lines-per-inch grid that form elements automatically align to when you move or resize them.

: Drag and Drop

Precedents

Precedents are **cells** that supply **values** to the **formulas** in other cells. If cell A1 contains the formula =B1+C1, then cells B1 and C1 are precedents. They must provide values before the formula in cell A1 can calculate.

Calculation order

When you rely on precedents to provide values, be aware of the order in which a spreadsheet calculates. If a precedent is below or to the right of a **dependent** cell, you might get incorrect results. When Microsoft Works calculates a spreadsheet, it calculates each cell in the first **column** from top to bottom, then calculates each cell in the second column from top to bottom, and so on.

: Dependents; ERR Message

P

Printing 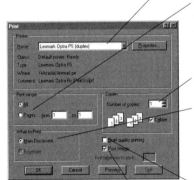 To print the **document** in the active **document window**, choose the File Print command. (If you've already made the appropriate settings in the Print dialog box, you can bypass it by clicking the Print tool.)

Before You Print

1 Create a document and then format it as desired.

2 Use the **Page Setup** dialog box to select a paper size, set **margins**, and so on.

3 Choose File **Print Preview** to see how your printed pages will look.

When You're Ready to Print

Choose the File Print command to display the Print dialog box.

Select a printer if you have more than one connected to your system.

If you don't want to print the whole document, select Pages and type the numbers of the first and last pages you want to print.

Type the number of document copies you want.

The What To Print section appears only when you print a word processor document that contains an envelope or mailing label.

Marking the Draft Quality Printing check box prevents charts, database forms, graphics, and different fonts from printing, which can speed up printing.

Mark the Print Merge check box if you want to replace a word processor document's field place-holders with the contents of database fields.

continues

Printing *(continued)*

If you don't want to print a complete document

Whenever you print a multipage document, you can specify a range of pages to print. But there are other ways to print part of a spreadsheet or database:

- To print only part of a spreadsheet, select the range of cells you want to print and then choose the Format Set Print Area command. (To reset the print area so the whole spreadsheet prints, choose Insert Range Name, select Print Area, click the Delete button, and then click Close.)

- To print certain records from a database, see **Hiding Records** to find out how to hide records you don't want to print. You can also print a single record in form view: Display the record and then select the Current Record Only radio button in the Print dialog box.

Envelopes; Mailing Labels; Mail Merge

Print Preview
Save a tree and a trip to the printer by previewing your documents on screen before you print them. Choose the File Print Preview command.

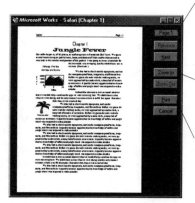

Works displays the page number of the currently displayed page. Click Previous or Next to flip through the pages.

Works starts the preview by displaying a full page. Click Zoom In for a closer look.

If everything looks OK, click Print. If you need to make corrections first, click Cancel—and pat yourself on the back for saving paper.

Protecting Cells 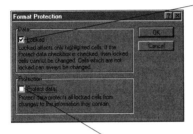 You can prevent changes to spreadsheet **cells** by protecting them. You can protect certain cells— ones that contain complex **formulas** or data that you don't want to change—and leave other parts of the document unprotected so you can enter new data. Protecting cells is a two-step process:

1 Lock the cells you want protected; unlock the cells you want to be able to change. You do this by selecting the cells you want to lock or unlock. Then choose the Format Protection command. Mark the Locked check box to lock (protect), or clear it to unlock the highlighted cells. Then click OK.

2 To enable the cell locking you have set, you must turn on protection. To do so, choose Format Protection and mark the Protect Data check box. Click OK.

Removing protection

When a document is protected, Works prevents you from changing the contents of locked cells. And it also disables many other commands that control **formatting**, add or delete rows or columns, and so on. To restore these capabilities, you must turn off protection. Choose Format Protection, clear the Protect Data check box, and click OK.

P

WORKS A TO Z

Protecting Fields You can prevent changes to the contents of certain database **fields** by protecting them. Follow these steps to protect fields:

1 Switch to **list view** or **form design view**.
2 Select the fields you want to protect.
3 Choose the Format Protection command.
4 Mark the Protect Field check box and click OK.

Protocol In Microsoft Works, protocol has nothing to do with the way you address the queen of England—unless you're sending files to her via modem. The error-checking method two modem-connected computers use to exchange files is called a protocol, and both computers must use the same protocol. Works supports four popular protocols: Zmodem, Ymodem, Xmodem/CRC, and Kermit. To select a protocol, follow these steps:

1 Choose the Settings Transfer command.
2 Select a protocol in the Transfer Protocol list box.
3 Click OK.

Which protocol to use?

Your choice is limited to the protocols supported by the computer you're communicating with. The list of protocols above shows them in order of desirability (i.e., speed, reliability, and features), so if the other computer supports more than one of the Works-supported protocols, select the best one supported by both computers.

⁘ **Sending and Receiving Files; Sending and Receiving Text**

Queries

❖ **Filtering Records**

Range  A range is a group of adjacent **cells**. You'll often find it necessary to refer to a range in **formulas**. To refer to a range, you specify the **cell addresses** of the upper left and lower right corners of the range, separated by a colon.

As indicated to the left of the **entry bar**, the address of the selected range is B4:D9.

❖ **Absolute Cell References; Mixed Cell References; Names; Relative Cell References**

Records A record contains the data for a single "thing" (whatever "things" your database tracks, such as customers, compact discs, or store inventory). Each record is divided into **fields**. In **form view**, a single record is displayed. In **list view**, each record occupies one row.

A Microsoft Works database can contain up to 32,000 records.

❖ **Adding Records; Deleting Records; Filtering Records; Hiding Records; Marking Records; Scrolling; Sorting Records**

Redo   If you change a document and then change your mind, choose the Edit Undo command. But if you change your mind again, choose the Edit Redo command, and your change is redone. You can continue this cycle endlessly if you like, but you'll probably tire of it quickly.

∴ **Undo**

Relative Cell References   A relative cell reference is a **cell address** that Works adjusts if it's part of a **formula** that you copy. By default, all cell references are relative unless you add dollar signs to make them absolute. Maybe this example will help:

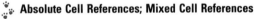

Unsaved Spreadsheet 1		
	A	B
1	5	
2	7	
3		2

Cell A2 contains the formula =A1+2. A1 is a relative reference.

If you copy the formula from cell A2 to cell B3, Works adjusts the formula in cell B3 to read =B2+2. When you copy the formula to the right one column and down one row, Works changes the address so that it still refers to the cell immediately above the formula cell.

∴ **Absolute Cell References; Mixed Cell References**

Replacing Cell or Field Contents 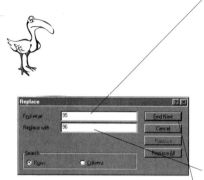 The Edit Replace command searches for **cells** or **fields** that contain the text, numbers, or formula that you specify and then replaces it. To use the Edit Replace command, follow these steps:

1 Select the **range** of cells or fields you want Works to search.

2 Choose the Edit Replace command.

3 In the Find What text box, type the characters you want to find. You can enter text, numbers, a **formula**, or part of a formula. Note that Works searches only the formulas in cells or fields—not the **values** produced by the formulas.

4 Type your replacement text in the Replace With text box.

5 Click Find Next. Works searches until it finds your text and then pauses.

6 Click Replace to replace the found occurrence or click Find Next to continue searching without replacing. If you're sure of yourself, click Replace All to find and replace all occurrences within the selected range.

Editing Cells; Editing Records; Finding Cells; Finding Records

121

Replacing Text 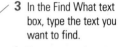 Choose the Edit Replace command to find text you specify and then—at your option—replace it with other text. To use the Edit Replace command, follow these steps:

1 Select the text you want to search. If you want to search the entire document, don't select any text.

2 Choose the Edit Replace command.

3 In the Find What text box, type the text you want to find.

4 Type your replacement text in the Replace With text box.

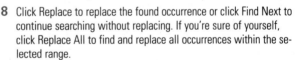

5 If you want Works to find only whole-word occurrences of the text, mark the Find Whole Words Only check box.

6 If you want Works to find only text that matches exactly, including capitalization, mark the Match Case check box.

7 Click Find Next. Works searches until it finds your text and then pauses.

8 Click Replace to replace the found occurrence or click Find Next to continue searching without replacing. If you're sure of yourself, click Replace All to find and replace all occurrences within the selected range.

⁂ **Editing Text; Finding Text**

Reports Reports provide a way to view and analyze your **database** in ways not possible with **form view** and **list view**. With a report, you can:

- Specify which fields to include and where to place them on the page—without modifying the database or its **form**

- Sort and group records based on field contents

- Perform calculations on fields and groups of records to provide summary information

- Add titles, headings, and other text to embellish the report

A report includes only records that are not hidden. You can use a filter to hide the records you're not interested in before you print a report.

Creating a Report

1 Choose the Tools ReportCreator command.

2 In the Report Name dialog box, type a name for your report. (This is the name by which you'll refer to this report; the name won't appear on the report.) Click OK.

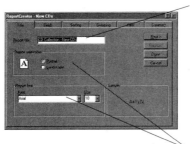

3 On the Title tab, type a title for your report. (The title appears at the top of the first page.) Works suggests the name of your database followed by the name of the report as a title, but you can change it if you like.

4 Specify a page orientation and a font for the report. Click Next >.

continues

Reports *(continued)*

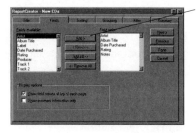

5 On the Fields tab, se-
lect each field you
want to include in the
report and click the
Add > button. When
you're done selecting
fields, click Next >.

6 On the Sorting tab, select the fields on which you want to sort your
records. If you select more than one field, Works sorts on the first
field, and for all records that have a common first field, Works
sorts on the second field, and so on. (If you don't specify fields for
sorting, your report displays nonhidden records in the same order
they appear in list view or form view.) Click Next >.

7 On the Grouping tab, you can set options for grouping records that
have the same contents in each of the sort fields you selected in
step 6. When you're done, click Next >.

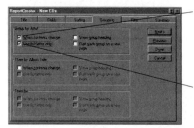

To group records that
have the same field
contents, mark the When
Contents Change check
box.

To group records by the
first letter of the field
(handy when printing
directories of names, for
example), mark the Use
First Letter Only check
box.

8 On the Filter tab, you specify which records you want to include in
the report. Select Current Records to include the currently displayed (that is, nonhidden) records; select All Records to include,
you guessed it, all records; select an existing filter; or click Create
New Filter. Then click Next >.

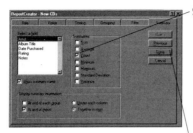

9 On the Summary tab, you can mark one or more calculations for each field in the report. Works places the results of the calculations at the end of each group or at the end of the report.

10 Click Done.

Works uses **report view** to display the report definition. You can modify the report by **inserting columns and rows**, **formatting**, entering text and **formulas**, and so on. Commands on the Tools menu let you change your sorting, grouping, and filtering options. To see the results of your report, choose the File **Print Preview** command. To print your report, choose File Print.

Reusing a Report

Works saves up to eight reports with a database document. (It automatically saves a report when you create it.) To reuse a report you've previously created, choose the View Report command, select the report name, and click Preview.

Deleting a Report

If you want to create a new report when the database already has eight reports, you must delete one. To do so, choose the Tools Delete Report command, select a report name, and click Delete. Click OK when you're finished deleting reports.

Filtering Records; Hiding Records; Page Setup; Printing

Report View  Report view shows your **report** definition. In report **view**, you can modify your report: add or delete columns or rows; add text, fields, or **formulas**; and format the output by adjusting **column width** or **row height, changing fonts**, and so on.

	A	B	C	D
Title		**My Extensive CD Collection**		
Title				
Headings	Artist	Album Title	Date Purchased	Rating
Intr Artist				
Intr Artist	=Artist			
Record		=Album Title	=Date Purchased	=Rating
Record		=Notes		
Record				
Summ Artist		="Number of "&Artist&" albums:"	=COUNT(Album Title)	
Summary				
Summary		COUNT OF Artist:	=COUNT(Artist)	
Summary		COUNT OF Album Title:	=COUNT(Album Title)	

Report Rows

A report definition uses several different types of rows; the type is identified at the left end of the row. When you use Insert Row to add a new row, Works asks which type of row you want to insert.

Type	What it does
Title	Prints at the top of the first page
Headings	Prints below the title on the first page, and at the top of all other pages
Intr *fieldname*	Appears at the beginning of each group if you sort and group records
Record	Prints fields from each record
Summ *fieldname*	Appears at the end of each group if you sort and group records
Summary	Prints at the end of the report

Resizing Fields

You must set **field** sizes in **form design view** and **list view** independently. Resizing a field in one view has no effect on the other.

Resizing a Field in Form Design View

1 Select the field you want to resize.

2 Drag one of the resizing handles.

Drag this handle to change the height.

Artist: MadKap

Drag this handle to change the width.

Drag this handle to change the width and the height simultaneously.

Do mice scare you?

Instead of dragging, you can choose the Format Field Size command (form design view) or the Format Field Width and Format Record Height commands (list view). Using the commands allows more precise sizing, and in list view the commands allow you to adjust multiple fields or records. Select the fields or records you want to resize before you choose a command.

Resizing a Field in List View

To adjust the width, move the mouse pointer to the border at the right side of the **field name** at the top of the column. Then drag the border to the desired width.

To adjust the height, drag the border below the record number at the left end of the row.

Making it fit

You can quickly adjust the width of a field in list view so that it perfectly contains the record with the longest field contents. Simply double-click the field name at the top of the column you want to adjust.

 Column Width; Row Height

Resizing Objects and Pictures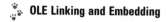
To change the size of an object or picture, click the object to select it. Then drag the sizing handles—the little gray squares along the object's borders.

Maintaining proportions

Drag one of the corner handles to change an object's size without distorting it.

🐾 **OLE Linking and Embedding**

Resizing Windows
To resize the Microsoft Works **application window** or one of its **document windows**, use the mouse to drag its border until it's the size you want.

Tidying up your workspace

Your **workspace** can get cluttered if you open several **documents**. You needn't close them to restore order. Minimize the ones you want "on the back burner" by clicking the minimize button (it looks like a line at the bottom of a window) in the document window's title bar. Then choose the Window Cascade or Window Tile command to neatly arrange the remaining open document windows.

🐾 **Control-Menu Commands**

Right-Clicking One of the neatest tricks in Windows 95 is the **shortcut menu**, which appears when you point at an object—a word, a picture, a cell, whatever—and click with the secondary mouse button. (That's usually the right button, unless you've changed it in Control Panel.)

Row Height You can change the height of a row with the mouse or with the Format Row Height command. (In database **list view,** use Format Record Height.)

Drag the border below the row number to change the height of that row.

The perfect row height

To adjust the row height to fit the tallest characters in the row, double-click the row number or click the Best Fit button in the Format Row Height dialog box.

Rows In **list view**, every database **record** occupies a row. You can apply anything you know about spreadsheet rows (such as how to adjust the **row height** or select rows) to records.

 Inserting Columns and Rows; Selecting Columns and Rows

Ruler

 The ruler, which appears at the top of each word processor **document window**, shows indents and tab settings. But the ruler is more than a pretty thing to look at: You can click the ruler to set a tab stop, or drag the indent and tab-stop markers to change the settings for the selected paragraphs.

To display the ruler if it isn't there—or to hide it if it's in your way—choose the View Ruler command.

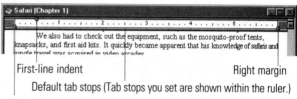

We also had to check out the equipment, such as the mosquito-proof tents, knapsacks, and first aid kits. It quickly became apparent that his knowledge of safaris and jungle travel was acquired in video arcades.

First-line indent   Right margin

Default tab stops (Tab stops you set are shown within the ruler.)

Left indent

⁂ Indents and Alignment; Options; Tabs

Saving Documents 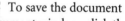 To save the document

that's displayed in the active document window, click the Save tool, press Ctrl+S, or choose the File Save command.

Saving a Document You've Already Saved

If the document has been saved before, Works promptly replaces the old version with the latest version.

Saving a Document for the First Time

If you're working on a new document, Works displays the Save As dialog box.

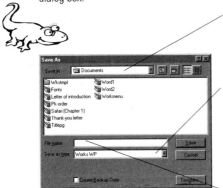

1 Select the disk drive and folder where you want to save the file. (Press F4 to open the Save In drop-down list.)

2 If you want to save the file in a format that can be read by another program, select that program in the Save As Type drop-down list box.

3 Type a **filename**. Works automatically appends the appropriate extension.

Changing a document's name

To change the name of a document that you've already saved, choose the File Save As command instead of File Save. Works then presents the Save As dialog box shown above, and you can type a new filename.

Exporting Documents

Saving the Workspace

You can save the name, window size, and window position of all open documents (including those that have been minimized) by saving the workspace. To do so, choose Tools Options and click the View tab. Then click Save Workspace. Then whenever you start Works, it automatically opens those documents and restores the window layout exactly as it was when you last saved the workspace.

continues

Saving the Workspace *(continued)*

When you don't want those documents any more

To change the saved workspace, simply rearrange it to fit your new needs and save the workspace again. But if you don't want to use the saved workspace feature at all, choose Tools Options and clear the Use Saved Workspace At Startup check box.

 Document Windows; Options

Scientific Notation When a cell with the general format contains a value that is too big or too small to fit in the cell's width, Microsoft Works uses **scientific notation**. In the illustration below, the **values** in column A are the same as those in column B; only the **column width** is different.

When it doesn't fit in the cell, Works displays the value 250,000,000 as 2.5E+08, which is equivalent to 2.5×10^8.

⚡ Unsaved Spreadsheet 2	
	A	B
1	250000000	2.5E+08
2	0.0000001	1E-07

The value 0.0000001 uses too many numbers to fit neatly in this cell, so Works displays it as 1E–07, which is equivalent to 1×10^{-7}.

If you wear a white lab coat

You might prefer to enter and view numbers in scientific notation. To enter a number in scientific notation, you can use either an uppercase or lowercase letter E, and you can omit the plus sign if the exponent is positive.

To be sure that numbers are displayed in scientific notation, choose Format Number and select Exponential. You can also specify the number of significant digits to display.

 **Formatting Numbers**

S

Scripts A script details the steps Works should take to perform a repetitive communications task, such as logging on to a service or downloading your new mail. Works can record your actions and save them as a script, and you can then modify the recorded script if you like.

Recording a Script

1 Choose the Tools Record Script command.

2 Select the Sign-on radio button to record a script that connects you to the other computer. Or select Other and type a name (15 characters or less) to record any other actions. Then click OK.

3 Perform all the steps necessary to complete the task.

4 Choose the Tools End Recording command.

Playing Back a Script

To play back your script, you simply choose its name from the Tools menu.

continues

Scripts *(continued)*

Modifying a Script

1 Choose the Tools Edit Script command.

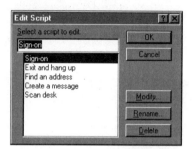

2 Select the name of the script you want to edit and then click the Modify button.

3 In the Script list box, select a command line you want to edit. Works displays an explanation of the command in the lower right corner.

You can edit or delete existing lines, or add new lines to your script.

Scrolling  Like most other Windows-based applications, Works displays vertical and horizontal scroll bars that let you move around within a document when the entire document doesn't fit within its window.

Click a vertical scroll arrow to move up or down by one line or row.

Click the scroll bar above the scroll box to move up one screenful, or below the scroll box to move down one screenful.

Drag the scroll box to move through the document; the box's size and position in the bar indicates your relative position in the document.

The horizontal scroll bar provides similar controls for moving horizontally.

The **document window** for a word processor document or database **form** includes another set of controls in its lower left corner.

Click to move to the beginning of the document (the first page or record).

Click to move to the previous page or record.

Click to move to the next page or record.

Click to move to the end of the document.

Go To; Window Panes

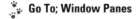

S

WORKS A TO Z

Selecting

Practically anything you do in Microsoft Works—copying, moving, editing, formatting—affects the *selection*, which is typically highlighted by changing its displayed colors to white text on a black background.

> Selecting cells in a spreadsheet or database list view ❖ **Selecting Cells; Selecting Columns and Rows**
>
> Selecting text ❖ **Selecting Text**
>
> Selecting embedded charts, pictures, notes, and so on ❖ **Selecting Objects**

Selecting multiple fields in a database form

You don't need to switch to **list view** to select more than one **field**. In **form design view,** you can point at the **form's** background and begin dragging; Works displays a dotted rectangle. Drag until you surround the fields you want to select. When you release the mouse button, all the enclosed fields are selected.

Selecting Cells

To select a single cell, click it or use the direction keys to move the **cell selector**, a heavy border that indicates the **active cell**.

To select a rectangular **range** of cells, drag the mouse from one corner of the range to the opposite corner. With the keyboard, move the active cell to one corner of the range, hold down the Shift key, and use the direction keys to move to the opposite corner. When you select a range, one cell—the one that is outlined but not reversed—is still the active cell.

A mouse shortcut for selecting a range

To quickly select a range of cells, click the cell in one corner of the range. Then hold down the Shift key and click the cell in the opposite corner.

❖ **Selecting Columns and Rows**

136

S

Selecting Columns and Rows  Click a **column**
letter or **row** number to select an entire column or row.
(In database **list view**, click the **field name** or **record**
number.) To select multiple columns or rows, drag from
the first column letter or row number in the range you
want to select to the last one.

Extending the selection

After you select a cell, a range, a row, or a column, you can
extend the selection to adjacent cells by holding the Shift key
and pressing a direction key.

> Selecting Cells

Selecting Objects  The easiest way to select an ob-
ject—an embedded **chart, table, Note-It** note, **ClipArt
Gallery** picture, what have you—is to click anywhere
within the object. You'll know it's selected because it
gains a gray border with little squares (called sizing
handles) in each corner and along each side. When the
object is selected, you can move it, copy it, change its size,
or delete it.

Once is enough

Use a single click to select an object. Double-clicking activates the
object's source application so you can edit or "play" the object.
(Whether a double-click edits or plays depends on the type of object,
and is determined by the object's source.)

> Copying Objects and Pictures; Deleting Objects; Moving
> Objects and Pictures; Resizing Objects and Pictures

Selecting Text ✏️ Selecting text in a word processor document is most easily done with a mouse, as shown in the following table.

To select	Do this
A word	Double-click the word
A line	Click in the left margin
A sentence	Hold Ctrl and click within the sentence
A paragraph	Double-click in the left margin
Entire document	Hold Ctrl and click in the left margin

If you prefer the keyboard, simply place the **insertion point** where you want to begin the selection, hold down Shift, and use direction keys to extend the selection.

Extending the selection

To select more than one word, line, sentence, or paragraph, take the action shown in the table above and then, without releasing the mouse button, drag to include adjacent words, lines, sentences, or paragraphs.

Sending and Receiving Files 📠 You can send a document (or any other type of file stored on your computer) to another computer. Similarly, you can receive a file sent from the other computer and save it directly to a disk file instead of having it appear in the document window.

Before you send or receive a file, find out what **protocol** the other computer uses, and set yours to match. Then make a connection with the other computer.

Sending a File

1 Choose the Tools Send File command.

2 When the Send File dialog box appears, select the drive, folder, and filename of the file you want to send.

3 Click Send.

Works signals the other computer that it's ready to begin sending a file and displays a dialog box that shows its progress. To stop a file transfer before it's finished, press Esc.

Receiving a File

1 Ask the operator of the other computer—or the other computer itself—to begin sending a file. With most online services, you initiate a file transfer by selecting a file to "download" and then sending a command that tells the other computer to begin the download.

2 Choose the Tools Receive File command.

3 The Receive File dialog box appears. If you are using the Xmodem protocol, type a filename and choose OK. (With the other protocols, Works automatically saves the files with the same name used on the original system.)

Works displays its progress in the Receive File dialog box. To cancel a file transfer before it's finished, press Esc.

Sending and Receiving Text

Sending and Receiving Text

When you send or receive text, it appears in the document window without any formatting. To send text after you've made a connection, you simply type. The text you type should appear on your screen and on the other computer's screen.

Sending Text from Another Document

If you want to send large chunks of text that you've already typed somewhere else, such as in another document, follow these steps:

1 In the other document, select the text you want to send.

2 Choose Edit Copy to copy the text to the **Clipboard**.

3 Switch to the communications document.

4 Choose the Edit Paste Text command.

Works sends the text to the other computer. And it does it a lot faster than I can type.

continues

Sending and Receiving Text *(continued)*

Sending Text from a File

You can also send text that has been saved in an **ASCII text file.**
Connect to the other computer and then follow these steps:

1 Choose the Tools Send Text command.

2 Select the name of the file that contains the text you want to send.

3 Choose OK.

What's the difference between "sending text" and "sending files"?

When I talk about sending or receiving text, I'm referring to the stuff
that appears in the communications document's window, which is usually
unformatted text. Unless you capture it to a file, this information disappears for-
ever when you close the communications document.

Files that you send or receive, on the other hand, don't appear in the document
window. They go directly between your disk and the other computer's disk. Although this type of file transfer is commonly used for **binary files**, you can send
or receive any type of file this way.

 Capturing Text; Sending and Receiving Files

Series

 Charts; Filling Cells; Fill Series

Shading

You can apply shading or predefined pat-
terns, such as parallel lines or tiny dots, to the background of spreadsheet **cells**; the background of database
fields, field names, labels, or **forms**; **chart components**;
or the background of **paragraphs** in word processor
documents. To do so, follow these steps:

1 Select the cells or fields that you want to color. (If you want to
shade the background of a database form, click in the background
so that no field is selected.)

2 Choose the Format Shading command.

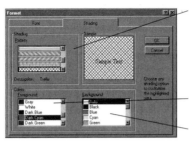

3 For a solid-colored background, select the solid bar in the Pattern list box (the first choice below None). Or select a pattern.

4 Select a color from the Foreground list.

5 If you selected a nonsolid pattern, you can select a back-ground color.

6 Click OK.

The colors you select are applied to the pattern you select from the Pattern list—not to the text in the selection.

What color is Auto?

The Auto color option uses colors that you set in Windows Control Panel (Display properties). The Window color is used as background, and the Window font color is used as foreground.

 Color

Sharing Works Data You can embed Works spreadsheets or **charts** into other applications that use **OLE linking and embedding**, such as Microsoft Word or WordPerfect for Windows. Follow these steps:

1 Select the spreadsheet **range** or chart you want to use.

2 Choose the Edit Copy command.

3 Switch to your other application and display the document you want to add the Works data to.

4 Use the other application's Edit Paste or Edit Paste Special command to embed the spreadsheet or chart in the document.

Clipboard; Exporting Documents

Shortcut Menus 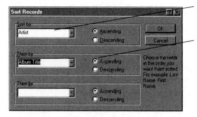 **Right-clicking** an object
displays a menu that includes commands that are appro-
priate for the object you're pointing to, so it usually saves
you a trip up to the menu bar at the top of the window.
(If the command you need isn't on the shortcut menu,
just move the mouse pointer to the menu bar and select
the command in the usual way.)

Sorting Records You can sort database records based on
the contents of up to three fields. You might use this to
arrange records in ZIP order before performing a mail
merge or just to change the order for viewing. To do so,
choose the Record Sort Records command.

Select the name of the
field you want to sort on.

Select the sort order:
ascending (A to Z, lowest
to highest, first to last) or
descending (the other
way!).

The Record Sort Records command sorts the entire
database, including hidden records.

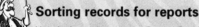

Sorting records for reports

You don't need to use the Record Sort Records command to produce a
sorted report. The report generator can sort (and also group) records
when it prepares a report.

∴ **Filtering Records; Finding Records; Reports**

Sorting Rows

You can sort the rows of a spreadsheet—or part of a spreadsheet—by choosing the Tools Sort command. Follow these steps:

1 Select the rows you want to sort. (Works always sorts entire rows, even if you select only partial rows.)

2 Choose the Tools Sort command.

3 Select the letter of the column you want to sort on.

4 Select the sort order: ascending or descending.

5 Click Advanced and repeat steps 3 and 4 to sort on additional columns.

6 Click Sort.

⁘ Selecting Columns and Rows

Special Characters

You can use the Insert Special Character command to insert **nonprinting characters.** If you use any of them frequently, you'll quickly learn its keyboard shortcut, which provides a faster, easier way to insert them.

To insert this character	You can use this shortcut key
End-of-line mark	Shift+Enter
Optional hyphen	Ctrl+hyphen
Nonbreaking hyphen	Ctrl+Shift+hyphen
Nonbreaking space	Ctrl+Shift+Spacebar

⁘ Ending Lines; Hyphenation; Nonbreaking Spaces; Symbols

Spelling Checker Works can check documents
for misspelled words. To use the spelling checker, first select the text or **cells** you want to proof. (If you want to
proof an entire document, don't select any text or select a
single cell.) Then choose the Tools Spelling command.
Works pauses when it finds a word that's not in its dictionary and displays the Spelling dialog box.

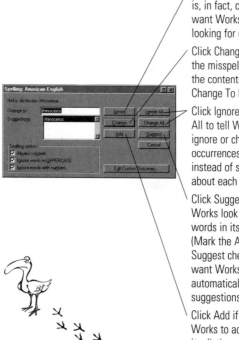

Click Ignore if the word
is, in fact, correct and you
want Works to continue
looking for other errors.

Click Change to replace
the misspelled word with
the contents of the
Change To box.

Click Ignore All or Change
All to tell Works to
ignore or change other
occurrences of the word
instead of stopping to ask
about each one.

Click Suggest to have
Works look for similar
words in its dictionary.
(Mark the Always
Suggest check box if you
want Works to
automatically make
suggestions.)

Click Add if you want
Works to add the word to
its dictionary.

Selecting a Dictionary

Dictionaries are available for other languages and for specialized
vocabularies, such as legalese. To select a dictionary that's been
installed on your system, choose the Tools Options command. Then
click the Proofing Tools tab and select a dictionary from the Choose
Dictionary list.

S

Checking databases and spreadsheets

In a database, the spelling checker proofs only the contents of the database **records**. It's up to you to find errors in **field names**, labels, or other text on database **forms**. The spelling checker also ignores cells and **fields** that contain **formulas**.

Spreadsheets  A spreadsheet is a document type that was inspired by accountants' ruled ledger forms. In its electronic rendition, a spreadsheet is a huge grid of **cells** in which you can enter numbers or **formulas** that perform calculations on the **values** in other cells.

New Documents

Spreadsheet View  When you are viewing a **chart**, you can switch back to the spreadsheet on which the chart is based by choosing the View Spreadsheet command. To switch to spreadsheet view from a chart embedded in a word processor document or database **form**, follow these steps:

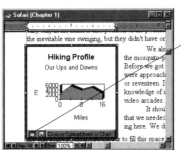

1 Double-click the chart to activate it.

2 Click the spreadsheet icon to switch to spreadsheet view. You can then modify the numbers that create the chart.

Views

Starting Works

You start Works by clicking the Microsoft Works icon on the Windows 95 Start menu. Follow these steps:

1 Click the Start button.
2 Select Programs, and then select Microsoft Works 4.0.
3 Click the Microsoft Works 4.0 icon.

You can also start Works by double-clicking its icon (or the icon for a Works document) on the desktop or in a folder window.

❖ Options; Saving the Workspace; Works Task Launcher

Statistical Functions

Works has seven statistical functions, which calculate the sum, average (mean), number, minimum or maximum value, standard deviation, or variance of a group of numbers. **Arguments** in the statistical functions can be **values** or cell references (including **range** addresses or **names**); separate the arguments with a comma. The following **formula** produces the sum of the values in each of the specified cells:

=SUM(B1:B12)

That's sum button

The easiest way to insert a formula that calculates the sum of a column or row of numbers is to click the **AutoSum** tool.

❖ Absolute Cell References; Easy Calc; Mixed Cell References; Relative Cell References

Status Bar

The status bar appears at the bottom of the Works **application window**. At its left end is a message area that offers helpful suggestions and describes each command as you highlight it.

The right end of the status bar shows information about the active **document**. When a word processor document is active, Works shows the number of the current page and the total number of pages. For a **database**, Works displays the number of the current **record**, the number of nonhidden records, and the total number of records in the database. During a communications session, Works displays the amount of time you've been connected.

Sandwiched in between are several indicators:

Indicator	What it means
CAPS	The keyboard's Caps Lock is on, which means that all letter keys type as capitals. Press the Caps Lock key to turn Caps Lock off.
NUM	The keyboard's Num Lock is on, which means the numeric keypad enters numbers. If you want to use its direction keys, hold down Shift. Or you can press the Num Lock key to turn Num Lock off.
OVR	Overtype mode is selected, which means that each character you type replaces the character to the right of the **insertion point**. To turn overtype mode off, press the Ins key.
CIRC	The spreadsheet contains a **circular reference**.
OFFLINE	You are not connected to another computer.
DIAL	The modem is making a connection.
PLAY	A recorded script is playing back.
REC	You are currently recording a communications script.

What status bar?

If your Works window doesn't have a status bar, choose the Tools Options command and then, on the View tab, mark the Show Status Bar check box.

Subtotaling Records
To perform calculations on groups of related database records, create a report.

Reports; Report View

Switching Windows Microsoft Windows and Works provide an ideal environment for people who like to jump from one fleeting thought to another because you don't need to finish one activity before you start something else. You can make any window the active window by clicking in it, or you can use one of these keystrokes:

To activate the next	Press
Window pane	F6
Document window	Ctrl+F6 or Ctrl+Tab
Application window	Alt+Tab

Symbols The Windows character set includes all the characters on your keyboard plus many special characters such as paragraph marks, bullets, mathematical symbols, and accented characters. These nonkeyboard characters are sometimes called extended characters.

You can use the Windows Character Map application to paste extended characters into your documents. To do so, click the Start button, choose Programs, and open the Accessories group. Then choose Character Map. Select the character you want and click Copy to place the character on the Windows **Clipboard**. Return to Works, and paste the Clipboard contents into your document.

I don't need a map! I never get lost!

You might find it inconvenient to switch to Character Map and back every time you want to insert a character. Windows lets you enter any character using the keyboard—but you must know the code! Each character is assigned a code number, which you use to enter the character. To see the code number for a character, select the character in Character Map and look at the "Keystroke" message in the status bar. To insert a character that is not on your keyboard, hold down Alt and type the character's code number using the numeric keypad. (You must type the code's initial zero, and you must use the numeric keypad; the number keys above the letter keys will not work.)

 Easy Text

Tables A table in a word processor document is like a
Works **spreadsheet** with only minor differences. (The
most visible differences are that column letters and row
numbers are not displayed—although you can still refer
to a table cell by its **cell address**—and you make entries
directly in the table cells instead of in the **entry bar**.) This
has its advantages: Unlike ordinary tabular text, Works
tables can perform calculations. (Of course, your table
doesn't have to contain numeric information.) And if
you know how to use the Works spreadsheet module, you
know everything there is to know about using tables.

Creating a Table

To create a table in a word processor document, follow these steps:

1 Place the **insertion point** where you want the table.

2 Choose the Insert Table command.

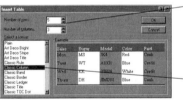

3 Specify the number of
rows and columns in
your table. (You can in-
sert or delete rows or
columns later.)

4 Select a format for
your table.

5 Click OK. Works embeds a spreadsheet-like table in your document.

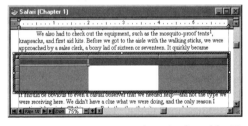

You can enter text or numbers in the table. Notice that,
while the table is active, the spreadsheet toolbar and
menus appear. (The table is active when it has a thick
border.)

continues

Tables *(continued)*

Using spreadsheet data as a table

If you want to insert data from an existing spreadsheet into your word processor document (or you want your table to have *all* the capabilities of a spreadsheet, including charting), choose Insert Spreadsheet instead of Insert Table when you create your table.

Modifying a Table

To activate an embedded table, double-click it. Click outside the table to return to the word processor text.

If you need to change the number of columns or rows, choose one of the commands on the Insert menu.

You can adjust the **column width** or **row height** for the entire table by dragging the sizing handles (the little squares along the table's border) to enlarge or reduce the table. You can adjust the size of individual columns or rows in the usual manner; often the best way is to double-click the gray box at the top of the column or left end of the row, which applies the "best fit."

Tabs

In Works, you can create different tab-stop settings in each **paragraph**. Even if you don't set any tab stops in a paragraph, Works uses its own default tab stops, which are normally set every half inch.

The **ruler** shows the tab-stop settings for the current paragraph (the one containing the **insertion point**) using these symbols:

Left (left aligns text)   Right (right aligns text)

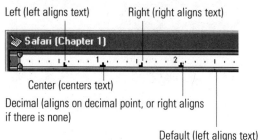

Center (centers text)

Decimal (aligns on decimal point, or right aligns if there is none)

Default (left aligns text)

Setting Tab Stops

1 Select the paragraph(s) in which you want to set tab stops.

2 Choose the Format Tabs command.

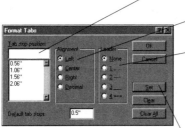

3 Type the position of the tab stop you want to add.

4 Select an alignment radio button.

5 Select a leader radio button if you want a dotted line or other character to fill the blank space before the tab stop.

6 Click the Set button.

7 Repeat steps 3 through 6 to set additional tab stops. Click OK when you're finished.

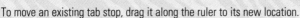

Using Tabs

Press the Tab key to insert a tab character, which moves the insertion point to the next tab stop, leaving a blank space in its wake.

Changing tab stops with the ruler and the mouse

To insert a left tab stop, click the ruler where you want the tab stop. To insert a tab stop with any other alignment (or with a leader character), double-click the ruler to display the Format Tabs dialog box.

To move an existing tab stop, drag it along the ruler to its new location.

To delete a tab stop, drag it off the ruler.

 Nonprinting Characters

TaskWizards  TaskWizards are helpers that can assist you in creating specialized databases, finding files, and other common tasks. They do so by asking you a series of questions (and showing by example what different answers will produce) and then performing all the necessary steps to complete the task. To use a TaskWizard (and to see a list and descriptions of the available wizards), choose File New and click the TaskWizards tab. Click a bold heading to view (or hide) the TaskWizards in a category, and then click a TaskWizard name to view its description. Click OK to run the selected TaskWizard.

‣ **Address Book TaskWizard; Templates**

Templates  A template is a document that already has some information and formatting in it. When you create a new document, a template gives you a head start compared with starting from a blank screen.

Creating a Template

1 Create the document you want to use as a template. (A blank letterhead or expense report, perhaps?) You can use a **TaskWizard**
to create the document.

2 Choose the File Save As command.

3 Click the Template button.

4 Type a name for your template and click OK.

Works adds your template to the User Defined Templates TaskWizard
group.

Using a Template

1 Choose the File New command to open the **Works Task
Launcher.**

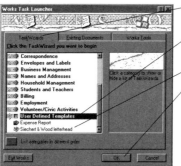

2 Click the TaskWizards
tab.

3 Select User Defined
Templates.

4 Select a template.

5 Click OK.

Assigning a default template

You can select a template for each Works module (word processor,
spreadsheet, database, and communications) to use as a default
template, which means that Works uses that template whenever you create a
new document. In the Save As Template dialog box, mark the Use This Template
For New *Module* Documents check box before you click OK.

Saving Documents

Terminal Settings The options in the Terminal Settings
dialog box control how Works displays text it receives
from another computer. To access this dialog box, choose
the Settings Terminal command.

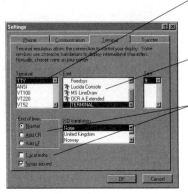

If the other computer
expects you to have a
specific type of terminal,
select it here.

You can select a different
font and size for text in the
communications window.

If text transmitted in a
communications session
overlaps, is double-
spaced, or doesn't appear
at all, tinker with the End
Of Lines, Local Echo, and
Wrap Around settings.
(See the Troubleshooting
section for more
information.)

Communication Settings; Phone Settings; Protocol

Text Columns To format your document into two or
more newspaper-style columns, choose the Format Columns command.

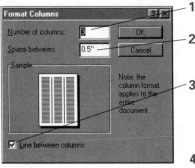

Note: the
column format
applies to the
entire
document.

1 Type the number of
   columns you want.

2 Type the amount of
   blank space to leave
   between columns.

3 Mark the Line Be-
   tween Columns check
   box if you want a vertical line to print be-
   tween columns.

4 Click OK.

To see the result of your change, choose the View Page Layout
command or use **print preview**.

Text Functions

 Microsoft Works includes 16 **functions** that, unlike all the other Works functions, operate on text instead of numeric **values**. With these text functions, you can format text with uniform capitalization, extract some text from a text string, remove blank spaces, and more. The following **formula** converts the text in cell B2 so that the first letter of each word is uppercase and all other letters are lowercase:

=PROPER(B2)

Arguments in a text function can be **cell addresses** or a text string enclosed in quotation marks, like this:

=EXACT("Match this!",B2)

(This formula returns TRUE if cell B2 contains the text *Match this!*, or FALSE if it contains anything else.)

∴ **Text String Formulas**

Text String Formulas

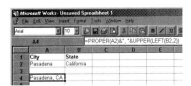 **Formulas** that operate on text strings can use **text functions** and they can use the & operator, which joins two text strings. In the illustration below, cell A4 contains the formula:

=PROPER(A2)&", "&UPPER(LEFT(B2,2))

This formula ensures that the city name (cell A2) is capitalized properly, appends a comma and a space, and then appends the capitalized first two letters of the state name (B2).

Thesaurus 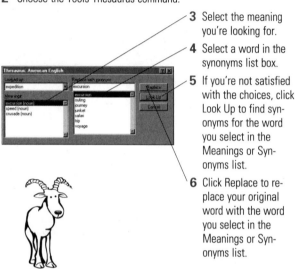 The thesaurus provides synonyms when you can't think of the right (correct, proper, perfect) word (expression, statement, locution). To use the thesaurus in Works, follow these steps:

1 Select the word for which you want to find a synonym.

2 Choose the Tools Thesaurus command.

3 Select the meaning you're looking for.

4 Select a word in the synonyms list box.

5 If you're not satisfied with the choices, click Look Up to find synonyms for the word you select in the Meanings or Synonyms list.

6 Click Replace to replace your original word with the word you select in the Meanings or Synonyms list.

Time Formats 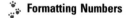 Using decimal values to represent times is useful for performing calculations, but if you want to see the **time values** in a format you can read (that is, a format that is recognizable as a time), follow these steps:

1 Select the cells that contain a time value.

2 Choose the Format Number command.

3 In the Format box, select the Time radio button.

4 In the Options box, select the format you want: 12-hour or 24-hour format, with or without seconds.

∴ **Formatting Numbers**

Times To insert into a word processor document the current time or the time when a document prints, choose the Insert Date And Time command.

Time Values Works uses decimal values to represent times, where each whole number represents 24 hours. 0 (or any whole number) represents 12:00 A.M., 0.25 represents 6:00 A.M., 0.5 represents 12:00 noon, and so on. This feature lets you perform calculations on time values (finding the elapsed time between two events, for example).

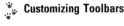 **Formulas; Time Formats**

Toolbars The toolbar is the row of graphical buttons right near the top of the Works **application window**. Clicking a toolbar button (a tool) is a shortcut for choosing a command from a menu. The toolbar changes, depending on what type of **document window** is active. To turn the toolbar display off (or back on), choose the View Toolbar command.

Slow down and it'll come to you

Some of the icons used on toolbar buttons don't exactly promote instant recognition. In fact, there's no telling what they are. But if you move the mouse pointer to a toolbar button and wait a few seconds, a ToolTip appears that tells what the tool does.

Customizing Toolbars

Transfer Settings

> :paw: **Protocol**

Underline Characters To <u>underline</u> characters, select the text (or the cells that contain the text) and then press Ctrl+U or click the Underline tool.

Undo

The Edit Undo command is the "Oops!" command. If you format some text, for example, and then decide that Wingdings is not a very legible font after all, choose Edit Undo. The Undo command can undo only your last action, so you must choose it before you make any other changes to your document.

> :paw: **Redo**

Values

A value is a number that you enter in a **cell** or a **formula**, and which can be used in arithmetic calculations performed by other formulas. Strictly speaking, a value can contain only digits (0 through 9), a decimal point (period), and a sign (+ or –). You can also use formatting characters (such as a dollar sign, comma, or percent sign), but Works doesn't retain them as part of the actual value.

> :paw: **Formatting Numbers; Percentages; Scientific Notation**

Views   Each Works module offers several ways to look at a document. To change views, choose the name of the view you want from the View menu, or click the appropriate **toolbar** button.

	Normal	Shows objects and actual fonts, but not in position
	Page Layout	Slower than normal view; shows everything in position—like **print preview**—except you can edit
	Wrap To Window*	Changes line endings to fit the **document window**; horizontal **scrolling** is unnecessary
	Chart	Shows spreadsheet information in a graphical format
	Spreadsheet	The basics: numbers on a grid
	Form	Displays a single **record** in a form-like layout
	List	Displays records in a spreadsheet-like window; each record occupies one row
	Form Design	Displays the form and allows changes to the form layout
	Report	Displays a **report** definition

* To obtain this view, choose View Normal. Then choose Tools Options and mark Wrap To Window on the Editing tab.

 Zooming

Window Panes

You can split the **document window** for a word processor document, spreadsheet, or database (**list view** only) into two panes, which allows you to look at different parts of the same document. You can scroll the information in each pane independently.

Splitting a Window into Two Panes

Drag the split bar—the tiny gap above the vertical scroll bar—down to divide the window into two panes. Alternatively, choose the Window Split command and click or press Enter when the split bar is where you want it.

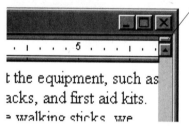

Split bar

In spreadsheets and databases, you can split the document window into four panes if you like. These windows have a vertical split bar in addition to the horizontal split bar.

To remove the split and restore a single-pane view, drag the split bar to the edge of the window.

Moving between panes isn't a pain

To place the **insertion point** in a pane, you click there. But you needn't take your hands off the keyboard to move to a different pane: Simply press F6 to move to the next pane.

 Scrolling

WordArt

WordArt is an accessory application that lets you create wacky distorted text. You can use it to create a logo or a heading in a word processor document or database **form**.

W

Creating a WordArt Object

1 Place the **insertion point** where you want the WordArt object to appear, and then choose the Insert WordArt command.

2 WordArt displays a new Enter Your Text Here window. Type the text that you want to use in your WordArt.

3 Choose the shape, font, and other effects you want using the WordArt **toolbar** and menu commands.

4 Click the Update Display button. If you don't like what you see, go back to step 3.

5 To close the Enter Your Text Here window, click its Close button or click anywhere else in the **document window**.

> Moving Objects and Pictures; OLE Linking and Embedding; Resizing Objects and Pictures

---

WordPad If you want to exchange word processor documents with people who have WordPad, the word processor that's included with Windows 95, use the File Save As command and select RTF or Word For Windows in the Save As Type drop-down list. To open a WordPad document in Works, choose File Open and select Word 6.0–7.0 For Windows & Macintosh in the Files Of Type list.

> Exporting Documents; Opening Documents; Saving Documents; Write

WordPerfect

WordPerfect is a word processor that's used by more people than the combined population of the countries of middle Africa. You can exchange documents with users of WordPerfect versions 5.0, 5.1, 5.2, 6.0, and 6.1 because Works can open and save documents in those formats.

> **Exporting Documents; Opening Documents; Saving Documents**

Word Wrap

Word wrap is the feature that moves a word to the next line when it doesn't fit on the current line. It might not sound like much—until you have an older person explain how typewriters worked in the olden days.

Doin' the word wrap

Normally Works wraps words based on the length of printed lines. In other words, your document appears on screen as it will when you print it. If you can't see complete lines on the screen, use the **zooming** feature to display more of the document or choose the View Normal command. Then choose Tools Options and mark the Wrap To Window check box on the Editing tab. Works then breaks lines to fit in the screen window—without affecting the way lines break when printed.

> **Ending Lines**

Workspace

The workspace is the part of the Works **application window** below the **toolbar**—the area where **document windows** appear.

> **Saving the Workspace**

W

Works Task Launcher

 The Works Task Launcher is your "control center" for Microsoft Works. It lets you create a new **document**, open an existing document, or use a **template** or **TaskWizard**. To open the Works Task Launcher, do one of the following:

- Start Works (unless you have saved the **workspace**, in which case Works displays the saved workspace instead).

- Click the Task Launcher tool.

- Choose the File New command.

- Close the only open **document window**.

Click the TaskWizards tab to see a list of TaskWizards and their descriptions

Click the Works Tools tab to open a new, blank document in any Works module

Click the Existing Documents tab to gain quick access to your eight most recently used documents, as well as other Works documents

Write  Write is a word processor that's included with Microsoft Windows version 3.*x*. Because every Windows user has a copy of Write or its Windows 95 replacement, **WordPad** (which can also read Write files), its format is convenient for exchanging documents with other users who don't have Works. But you don't have to use Write. Works can open and save word processor documents in Write format; simply choose Windows Write from the file-type list when you open or save a document.

∴ **Exporting Documents; Opening Documents; Saving Documents**

Zooming  Like a camera's zoom lens, Works can "zoom in" to give you a magnified view of the active document. Zooming enlarges or reduces the size of characters on the display, but it does not affect printed output. To zoom, click the zoom percentage shown at the bottom of the window.

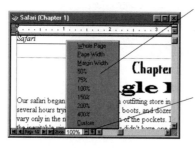

Select a magnification factor from the list, or select Custom and type a custom magnification from 25% through 1000% of normal size.

Click the + or – buttons to step up or down to the next predefined zoom level.

∴ **Print Preview; Views**

TROUBLE-SHOOTING

● ●

Got a problem? Starting on the next page are solutions to the problems that can plague users of Microsoft Works for Windows 95. You'll be on your way—and safely out of danger—in no time.

COMMUNICATIONS

You Can't Access
a Modem

If Works displays a message such as "Can't place a call on this TAPI line," it means that another program is using the modem or you've selected the wrong COM port for your modem.

Close other communications programs

1 If you have an active connection in another Works communications document, switch to its window and choose the Phone Hang Up command.

2 Be sure you aren't using another program that's accessing the modem, such as The Microsoft Network or a program that checks your remote electronic mail. Close such a program. If you use Microsoft Fax to receive faxes, click the Fax icon in the taskbar. Choose the Options Modem Properties command, and in the Answer Mode box, select Manual or Don't Answer. Then click OK.

Check your modem setup

Choose the Settings Modem command and then select a modem. If none is shown, click Add. Works tests each COM port in your system and finds which ones have a modem attached.

 Communications Settings

The Communications
Window Displays
"Garbage"

Don't take offense if the text in the communications window looks like a cartoon-character expletive.

Match the communication settings

1 Find out from the operator of the online service or computer you want to connect to what communications settings (baud rate, data bits, parity, and stop bits) to use.

2 Choose Settings Communication, click Properties, and set each item to match the other computer.

 Communications Settings

The Text in the Communications Document Window Isn't Right

Most systems that you connect to use similar conventions about which characters they send to your terminal, how they handle line endings, and so on. But not all of them. Choose the Settings Terminal command to solve the following problems.

If lines overprint or are double spaced

If each new line of text in a communications window displays right over the previous line, select Add LF in the End Of Lines box.

If a blank line appears between each line of text, select Normal in the End Of Lines box.

Characters appear twice or not at all

If every character you type appears twice, clear the Local Echo check box. If characters you type don't appear at all, mark the Local Echo check box.

Characters overprint at right end

If characters "pile up" at the right end of the line, mark the Wrap Around check box.

 Terminal Settings

Pasting Text Doesn't Work

Sometimes when you choose Edit Paste Text to send text from the Clipboard, the other computer can't keep up—and it doesn't correctly receive all the text.

Increase the line delay

1 Choose the Settings Transfer command.

2 Increase the number in the Line Delay box, which represents the time (in tenths of a second) that Works pauses at the end of each line to give the other computer a chance to catch its breath.

 Sending and Receiving Text

The Phone Dialer
Doesn't Work

If you get an error message when you choose
the Tools Dial This Number command,
you're probably missing a key Windows 95
component: Phone Dialer.

Install Phone Dialer

1 Click the Start button, select Settings, and select
Control Panel.

2 Double-click the Add/Remove Programs icon.

3 Click the Windows Setup tab.

4 Select Communications and click Details.

5 Mark the Phone Dialer check box.

6 Click OK two times.

Dialing Phone Numbers

DATABASE

You Can't Change the
Field Entries in
a Database

Works lets you protect certain fields from
changes. (This is especially handy for protecting a field that contains a formula, for example.) But if you're sure you want to change
the contents of a protected field, you can.

Remove data protection

If you want to remove protection from a certain field
without endangering other fields, follow these steps:

1 Select the field(s) you want to unprotect.

2 Choose Format Protection.

3 Clear the Protect Field check box and click OK.

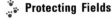

Protecting Fields

You Can't Make
Changes to a
Database

When you use **form view,** Works prevents you
from making many changes to a database.
Adding fields and **formatting numbers** is
prohibited, and you can't change **field
names,** add **headers and footers,** or have any
other fun.

Switch to form design view

Choose View Form Design to switch to **form design view**.

East Coast ZIP Codes
Lose Their
Leading Zero

Normally, Works drops zeros at the beginning of a number. But in some cases, such as for ZIP codes, those zeros are significant.

Use leading zero format

1 Select the field you want to format.

2 Choose the Format Field command.

3 Select Number. In the Appearance box, select 01235 and enter a Number Of Digits. (Use 5 for a ZIP code.)

Formatting Numbers

DOCUMENTS

You Can't Find a
Document

If you move or delete a document and then select it in the recently used files list in the **Works Task Launcher**, Works reports that it can't find the document.

Use the Works Task Launcher

If the document has been renamed or moved to another directory, click Help Me Find A Document to find it.

If the document you want has been deleted, you may be able to recover it by following these steps:

1 Click Cancel to close the Works Task Launcher.

2 Right-click the taskbar and choose Minimize All Windows to display the Windows desktop.

3 Double-click the Recycle Bin icon.

4 Find the deleted document in the Recycle Bin, and then choose File Restore.

5 Close the Recycle Bin window and switch back to Works.

6 Choose File Open to open the restored document.

Finding Files

New Documents
Already Contain
Information

Works allows you to create **templates**—documents that contain formatting information and text that you want to appear in every document based on the template. Works also allows you to designate one template as the default template for each module—and there's the rub. Whenever you create a new document, Works uses the default template.

Remove the default template

1 Choose File Save As.

2 Click Template.

3 Click Defaults.

4 Click Clear.

5 Click Cancel.

You Can't Open
a Document

Works does not allow a document to be open in more than one window or to be open by more than one person at a time.

Split the window

If you already have a document open in another Works window and you're trying to view different parts of the same document, split the window into two panes instead of trying to open a second document window.

Close the open document

If you want to open a document that's already open in another application on your computer or open by someone on another computer, you'll have to close the document before you can open it in Works.

 Closing Documents; Window Panes

PRINTING

Pages Don't Break
Where You Want

Works considers several factors when it de-
cides where to put page breaks: page size,
page orientation, margins, restrictions on
paragraph breaks, and manual **page breaks**
that you insert.

Insert a manual page break

1 Place the insertion point (or select the row or column) where you want a page break.

2 Choose the Insert Page Break command.

Save a tree!

To find out where pages break without wasting paper, choose
Print Preview.

The Printout Uses
the Wrong Font and
Graphics Don't Print

Works has a nifty feature that lets you print
faster by avoiding font changes and not printing graphics. This feature can cause dismay if
it's not what you expect, however.

Don't use the draft printing feature

Choose the File Print command and clear the Draft Quality Printing check box.

Field Placeholders
Print Instead of
Merge Data

To merge information from a database into a
word processor document, you insert a placeholder—the field name surrounded by « and
» symbols—in the document. But that's not
what you want to see when you print.

Use the print merge feature

Choose the File Print command and mark the Print
Merge check box.

 Mail Merge

Only Part of a
Spreadsheet Prints

The print area is set incorrectly. Change the
print area to the entire spreadsheet.

Reset the print area

1 Choose Edit Select All.

2 Choose Format Set Print Area.

You Can't Get
Gridlines to Print

Gridlines—those lines that separate the **cells**
in a spreadsheet or **fields** in database **list view**
—can be prevented from displaying and printing. But the View Gridlines command, which
controls the display, does not affect printing.

Change the page setup

1 Choose the File Page Setup command and select the
Other Options tab.

2 Mark the Print Gridlines check box if you want
gridlines to print; clear it if you don't.

SPREADSHEETS AND TABLES

Formulas Don't
Calculate Correctly

If a **formula** doesn't calculate the way you expect it to, it's probably a matter of "operator
precedence," which means that certain operators (an operator, such as a plus sign, specifies
what Works should do with the values on either side) are evaluated first—no matter
where they occur in a formula. You can control the order of calculation with parentheses:
Enclose the part of a formula that you want to
calculate first within parentheses.

Works Doesn't
Recognize Your
Entry as a Formula

If you enter a **formula** and Works displays the
formula in the cell instead of the **value** produced by the formula, you probably forgot
one little thing: You must start each formula
with an equal sign (=).

Edit the formula

1 Select the formula that's not a formula.

2 Press F2 to edit.

3 Press the Home key to move to the beginning of the formula, type an equal sign, and press Enter.

You Can't Enter Anything into a Cell

Works lets you protect certain cells from changes, which is handy for protecting formulas. But if you're sure you want to change the contents of a protected cell, you can.

Remove data protection

To remove protection from all cells, choose Format Protection and clear the Protect Data check box.

If you want to remove protection from a certain cell without affecting other cells, follow these steps:

1 Select the cell(s) you want to unprotect.

2 Choose Format Protection.

3 Clear the Locked check box and click OK.

 Protecting Cells

You Can't Display Long Text Entries

If a label or text entry won't fit within a column, Works lets it spread into adjacent cells on the right—until it runs into a cell that isn't empty.

Increase the column width

Double-click the column letter or field name to adjust the **column width** to fit the text.

Wrap the text onto multiple lines

1 Select the cell that won't fit.

2 Choose the Format Alignment command.

3 Mark the Wrap Text check box.

Values Display as

If a number or date is too wide to fit in a column, Works displays pound signs instead. The **value** in the cell is still there (and calculations are not affected); you just can't see it.

Increase the column width

Double-click the column letter or field name to adjust the **column width** to fit the column's contents.

Change the formatting

Select the offending cell and then choose the Format Number command. Select a format that requires less space: Eliminate unnecessary decimal places, commas, dollar signs, and so on. Or select General format.

Alternatively, you can select a smaller font size from the toolbar's point-size drop-down list.

 Formatting Numbers

WORD PROCESSOR

Tabular Text Doesn't Align Properly

If you use spaces to separate columns of text or to indent text from the left margin, the lines probably won't align vertically when you print.

Use indents, tabs, or tables

Instead of using spaces to move text to the right, use paragraph indents to adjust the left **margin**, and use **tabs** to set additional positions in a line where you want text to line up. And if you're setting up a **table**, the best way is to choose the Insert Table command.

QUICK REFERENCE

Any time you explore some exotic location, you're bound to see flora and fauna you can't identify. To make sure you can identify the toolbar buttons you see in Microsoft Works, the Quick Reference describes these items in systematic detail.

File Menu Tools

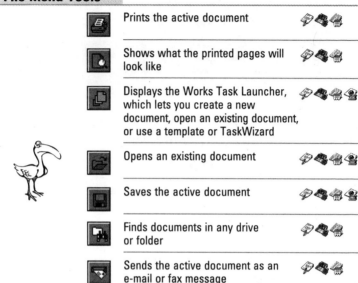

Prints the active document

Shows what the printed pages will look like

Displays the Works Task Launcher, which lets you create a new document, open an existing document, or use a template or TaskWizard

Opens an existing document

Saves the active document

Finds documents in any drive or folder

Sends the active document as an e-mail or fax message

Edit Menu Tools

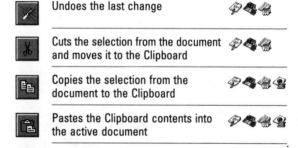

Undoes the last change

Cuts the selection from the document and moves it to the Clipboard

Copies the selection from the document to the Clipboard

Pastes the Clipboard contents into the active document

Deletes the selection without changing the Clipboard contents

What? No toolbar?

If your Works display doesn't include a toolbar right below the menu bar, choose the View Toolbar command.

	Inserts a bookmark	
	Finds text in the active document	
	Jumps to a specific place in the active document	
	Copies values, formats, and formulas from the leftmost selected cells to the selected cells to the right	
	Copies values, formats, and formulas from the topmost selected cells to the selected cells below	
	Fills selected cells with a series of numbers or dates	
	Edits legend or series labels	
	Jumps to the first data series in the spreadsheet	

Have it your way

Late one night, wired on pizza and soda, the Works programmers voted on their favorite toolbar buttons, and those are the ones included in the default toolbar for each module. This Quick Reference shows *all* the available toolbar buttons. If you find a button here that is not on the default toolbar and that performs an action you use frequently, see **Customizing Toolbars**.

View Menu Tools

	Wraps the text to fit in the window	
	Displays the active document in page layout view	
	Displays the active document in normal view	

continues

View Menu Tools *(continued)*

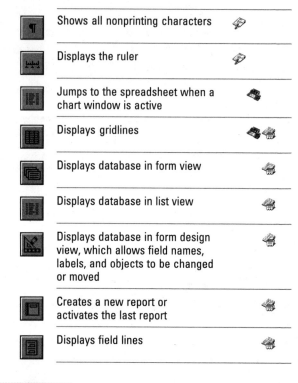

¶	Shows all nonprinting characters	
	Displays the ruler	
	Jumps to the spreadsheet when a chart window is active	
	Displays gridlines	
	Displays database in form view	
	Displays database in list view	
	Displays database in form design view, which allows field names, labels, and objects to be changed or moved	
	Creates a new report or activates the last report	
	Displays field lines	

Record Menu Tools

	Applies an existing filter	
	Displays all records	
	Displays hidden records and hides visible records	

ToolTips are sharp

When you leave the mouse pointer poised over a toolbar button, a little window pops up that tells you what the button does. The little window is called a ToolTip; if you want to test your iconic memory skills, choose the Tools Customize Toolbar command and deselect Enable ToolTips. (You can still look to the status bar for a more verbose description.)

	Hides selected records	🐘
	Inserts a blank record into the database	🐘
	Deletes selected records	🐘
	Inserts a field into the database	🐘
	Sorts records in ascending order (A to Z)	🐘
	Sorts records in descending order (Z to A)	🐘

Insert Menu Tools

	Inserts a page break	📝 🐢 🐘
	Inserts a footnote	📝
	Inserts a database field	📝
	Inserts the current date	📝
	Inserts the current time	📝
	Inserts Easy Text	📝
	Creates a chart	📝
	Inserts a Draw drawing	📝 🐘
	Inserts a Note-It note	📝 🐘
	Inserts a ClipArt Gallery picture	📝 🐘

continues

179

Insert Menu Tools *(continued)*

	Inserts a WordArt object	
	Inserts a table	
	Names the selection	
	Inserts a function on the entry bar	
	Inserts the SUM() function	
	Inserts blank rows above the selection	
	Inserts blank columns to the left of the selection	
	Deletes selected rows	
	Deletes selected columns	

Format Menu Tools

	Displays data as a simple area chart	
	Displays data as a simple bar chart	
	Displays data as a simple line chart	
	Displays data as a simple pie chart	
	Displays data as a stacked line chart	
	Displays data as a scatter chart	
	Displays data as a radar chart	

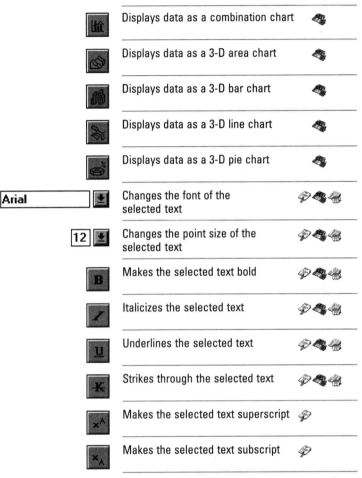

		Displays data as a combination chart	
		Displays data as a 3-D area chart	
		Displays data as a 3-D bar chart	
		Displays data as a 3-D line chart	
		Displays data as a 3-D pie chart	
Arial		Changes the font of the selected text	
12		Changes the point size of the selected text	
	B	Makes the selected text bold	
		Italicizes the selected text	
	U	Underlines the selected text	
	K	Strikes through the selected text	
	x^A	Makes the selected text superscript	
	x_A	Makes the selected text subscript	

continues

Font-selection tools

The procedure for including the font and point size list boxes on the toolbar is not the same as the procedure for including toolbar buttons. To include them, choose the Tools Customize Toolbar command and deselect Remove Font Name And Point Size From The Toolbar.

Format Menu Tools *(continued)*

Tool	Description	
☰	Aligns selected paragraphs at the left indent	🖱️💻🖨️
☰	Centers selected paragraphs between the left and right indents	🖱️💻🖨️
☰	Aligns selected paragraphs at the right indent	🖱️💻🖨️
☰	Aligns selected paragraphs at the left and right indents	🖱️
📄	Applies Easy Formats to the current selection	🖱️
└	Sets a left-aligned tab	🖱️
⊥	Sets a center-aligned tab	🖱️
┘	Sets a right-aligned tab	🖱️
⊥.	Sets a decimal-aligned tab	🖱️
☰	Formats the selected paragraphs as a bulleted list	🖱️
⇐	Decreases the left indent for the selected paragraphs by one-half inch	🖱️
⇒	Increases the left indent for the selected paragraphs by one-half inch	🖱️
☰	Sets line spacing for the selected paragraphs to one line	🖱️
☰	Sets line spacing for the selected paragraphs to two lines	🖱️
▦	Sets the column format for the active document	🖱️
▢	Positions a selected object in-line or by absolute measurement	🖱️

☐	Adds a border around the selected paragraphs, cells, or chart	
☐	Applies predefined formats to a table	
$	Applies currency format to the selection	
%	Applies percent format to the selection	
,	Applies comma format to the selection	
	Centers cell contents across selected columns	
	Freezes rows and columns before the selection as titles	
🔒	Protects data from changes	
	Sets selected cells as the area to print	
	Aligns fields to a grid	
	Shows the field name	

Settings Menu Tools

	Changes modem commands	
	Changes communication settings	

continues

Settings Menu Tools *(continued)*

	Changes terminal emulation	
	Changes phone options	
	Changes file-transfer options	
	Turns local echo on or off	
	Turns wrap around on or off	
8,n,1	Changes communication settings to 8,1,N,P	
7,e,1	Changes communication settings to 7,1,E,P	

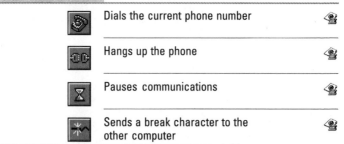

Phone Menu Tools

	Dials the current phone number	
	Hangs up the phone	
	Pauses communications	
	Sends a break character to the other computer	

Tools Menu Tools

	Checks spelling of the selection	
	Finds synonyms for the selected word	
	Counts the words in the selection	
	Creates envelopes or mailing labels	
	Dials the selected number	
	Opens the default address book	
	Launches the Works forum on The Microsoft Network	
	Creates a chart	
	Starts Easy Calc	
	Creates, deletes, renames, modifies, and applies filters	
	Calculates formulas in the active document	
	Captures incoming text in a file	
	Sends a file	
	Sends a document as a binary file	
	Receives a binary file	
	Records your actions as a script	

Window Menu Tools

 Arranges the open windows in an overlapping cascade

 Arranges the open windows in nonoverlapping tiles

 Places the icons for minimized windows at the bottom of the workspace